Also by Claude "Butch" Harmon, Jr.:

The Four Cornerstones of Winning Golf

BUTCH HARMON'S
PLAYING LESSONS

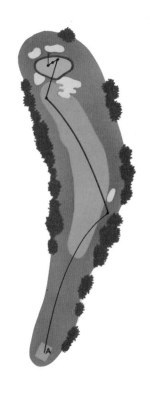

Claude "Butch" Harmon, Jr.
with John Andrisani

A FIRESIDE BOOK
PUBLISHED BY SIMON & SCHUSTER

FIRESIDE
Rockefeller Center
1230 Avenue of the Americas
New York, NY 10020

First Fireside Edition 1999

FIRESIDE and colophon are registered
trademarks of Simon & Schuster Inc.

Designed by Bonni Leon

Manufactured in the United States of America

1   3   5   7   9   10   8   6   4   2

The Library of Congress has cataloged the Simon & Schuster edition as follows:
Harmon, Claude, 1943–
Butch Harmon's playing lessons / Claude "Butch" Harmon, Jr., with John Andrisani.
p.   cm.
Includes index.
1. Golf—Study and teaching.   2. Golf courses—United States.
I. Andrisani, John.   II. Title.
GV962.5.H37   1998
796.352'3—dc21   97-52569
CIP

ISBN 0-684-83310-7
ISBN 0-684-85311-6 (Pbk)

ACKNOWLEDGMENTS

I would like to especially thank three people for bringing *Butch Harmon's Playing Lessons* to fruition: Jeff Neuman, my editor at Simon & Schuster, who helped me hatch the idea for writing this book; Scott Waxman, my agent; and John Andrisani, my co-writer, who always seems to get the job—of organizing the text, illustrations, and photography—done, and done right.

I'm grateful to Leonard Kamsler, particularly for his color photographs of the holes and for his instructional "takes." I also thank Allen Welkis, for doing such a nice job on all the drawings in this book.

I also thank my brothers, Craig, Dick, and Bill, who are all golf professionals, for sharing their knowledge on course strategy, the swing, and shotmaking technique with me.

Last, but surely not least, I thank Claude Harmon, Sr., the old master, who set me along the road of teaching golf. Thank you, Dad; you will forever be in my heart.

CONTENTS

INTRODUCTION

My first book, *The Four Cornerstones of Winning Golf*, concentrated on four main areas: ball striking; the short game; the mental side of golf, including course management; and physical conditioning. Almost all of the instructional tips I presented in the book were given to me by my dad, and so the book was also partly autobiographical. I told readers how my dad and I each evolved in the golf world, and I relayed the story of my dad's proudest moment, when he won the 1948 Masters as an underdog; club professionals are not supposed to win major championships.

In addition to describing the cornerstones in detail, I also analyzed the swings of Tiger Woods, Davis Love III, and Greg Norman, three players I had helped rebuild their swings. I wanted to show how easily faults can sneak into even a pro's swing and how easily they can be ironed out. Further, I showed how, just by making minor changes in the swing, a player's shotmaking—and his scores—can sometimes improve virtually overnight.

I now want to take the improvement process literally to the grass-roots level. In the course of this book, I take an A, a B, and a C player out on the course with me, and teach them how to play strategically smart golf that's right for their games and also teach them new shots, correct their faults, offer them drills for improvement, and lots more.

The course we play on is composed of 18 of America's best holes—in my book anyway. We tee off at the first hole at Shinnecock Hills in Southampton, Long Island, and finish the round again near New York City, playing the Westchester Country Club's 18th hole. There's a good mix of par-3, par-4, and par-5 holes on our course, including the 12th at Augusta National, the 14th at

Muirfield Village, and the 11th at the Tournament Players Club. Whether you've played these courses and the others of our layout already, or never play them in your lifetime, doesn't really matter; these holes are so famous that almost all modern designers have built similar holes. The situations that the players in my fictitious group run into are ones that you will face on your local course or on one you will visit.

What I suggest you do is match yourself up with either Player A, Player B, or Player C, and see how you would play the hole differently, or what you can learn from his experiences. Player A is an 8 handicap who hits solid tee shots 250 yards, a 5-iron 175 yards. If you're a single-digit player yourself, you will be able to relate well to his game. Player B's handicap is 14, his average drive is 230 yards, and his average 5-iron flies 160 yards. If your handicap falls between 10 and 16, you pretty much play the same game he does. Player C plays off a 22 handicap, drives the ball 210 yards, and hits 5-iron shots about 145 yards. In all cases, if these players take one more club, they hit it 10 yards father; one less club, 10 yards shorter. In other words, Player A hits a 6-iron 165 yards, a 4-iron 185 yards.

Player A is, of course, the best shotmaker of the group, but as you'll see, he, like the others, learns a lot during this round. Player B hits the ball a fair distance and has a basic understanding of the game, but makes some silly mistakes—namely, in club selection and in shotmaking choices. Player C, like most high-handicappers, has great potential, but he lacks power and needs to learn how to read lies better and play more shots. A little help in these areas can pay immediate dividends.

From tee to green, I offer tips on the total game: everything from where and how to aim, how to hit a power-draw, how to hit out of a divot, how to play from a buried lie in sand, to how to pace a long putt to the hole. Photographs and drawings are included to give you a better understanding of the hole itself or the instructional message I'm trying to relate.

Since the handicaps of the three players vary so much, you'll be treated to a wide range of shots. Personally, I think the entire book can serve as a refresher course for even the most experienced player.

Although I offer advice and constructive criticism along the way, it's at the end of each hole, in the section called *Butch's Lessons*, that I analyze each player's mistakes and tell him how to improve.

On the day of our game, Player A shot 76, Player B shot 84, and Player C shot 89, and I like to think I had something to do with that.

Let's see if I can't shave some numbers off your score.

BUTCH HARMON
Las Vegas, Nevada

Hole 1
SHINNECOCK HILLS
Par 4: 366 yards

Shinnecock Hills, located near the eastern tip of Long Island and about 90 miles from New York City, is one of the most historic venues in American golf. This magnificent layout, originally designed by emigrant Scotsman Willie Dunn in 1891, features relatively open land, tight springy turf, penal bunkering, and punishing golden rough, all of which make the playing experience here the closest to being in Scotland that anyone on these shores could hope for.

Shinnecock played host to the second U.S. Open in 1896, and although it hosted many other significant amateur events, the U.S. Open did not return until 90 years later, in 1986. Ray Floyd's winning one-under-par total of 279 that year and Corey Pavin's even-par 280 when the Open returned in 1995 are testament to the quality of this classic test.

The 1st hole has been assessed by many as a perfect opening hole. At first glance, the hole is not remarkable. At a length of 366 yards, and from an elevated tee that adds about 10 yards to the average tee shot, it can be a drive and an easy pitch for the expert player, and it's within easy reach in two shots by almost everybody. But it's still a great opening hole for a number of reasons. As you look out from the elevated tee over a wide vista that encompasses much of the great course, your appetite for an outstanding golfing experience is heightened. But beyond that, the fact that the 1st hole is not super difficult is a plus; no amateur golfer looks forward to playing a 470-yard 1st hole that has an out of bounds on both sides, where he knows if he doesn't spank a perfectly straight, long drive on his first swing of the day, he's looking at a big number. I believe both amateur and pro players appreciate a starting hole that eases them into their round, where good strategy and execution get them started with a par, maybe even a birdie, but which has some subtlety to it, too, so that bogeys are a distinct possibility.

The 1st at Shinnecock is that kind of hole—an inviting hole, but a bit of a teaser. The fairway doglegs right, and the tendency is to try to favor the right side of the fairway with the drive to shorten the hole. However, a fairly large fairway bunker lurks in the landing zone on the right, along with some generally ferocious rough. Also, remember that you'll rarely play Shinnecock Hills without having to cope with a fair amount of wind. The 1st fairway is relatively narrow, and the fact that you're trying to hit it from an elevation makes it particularly difficult when the wind is blowing.

The green is guarded by sand at front left and right, and is none too big. Also, the green is firm, so the ball doesn't bite that quickly, particularly on a day when the wind is behind you. Add a downslope at the left and rear of the green, and it presents an approach shot that smart players will view with caution rather than boldness. To sum up, while not punishing, the 1st at Shinnecock is a great opener that calls for controlled shotmaking by all three levels of players. Let's look at how each should attack number 1 or a hole very similar to it.

The A Player

Perhaps the most important factor on this hole, for a player like you who consistently shoots in the 70s, is to take the club that gives you the best chance to put your tee shot in the fairway. It's not really important that you hit a powerful drive, because even if you hit just a decent tee shot with any of your longer clubs, you'll be left with a manageable distance to the flag. But to have that birdie chance you have to put it in the fairway first.

You might think, okay, if my top priority is putting my drive in the fairway, I'll go with my 5-wood because that's the club I always feel I can hit the fairway with. But on this hole, the club choice for your tee shot is a little more complicated for two reasons: The tee's high elevation makes the shot vary greatly depending on the wind direction; and the hole is not so short that you can get away with a weak tee shot.

Suppose the hole is playing with a wind behind you of 10 to 15 miles per hour. In this case, your 5-wood is probably a perfect choice. If you normally hit this club 220 yards off the tee, and the ball flies high, it will get a 15-yard boost from the wind. Add to this the fact that the elevated tee gives you a 10-yard advantage, and a well-executed 5-wood shot will travel 245 yards. That sounds like a long way for a 5-wood, but this is a great example of the fact that you need to know the *true* distances your shots fly in the air, with various clubs in varying conditions. Most amateurs, even the best ones, fall into the trap of thinking they hit a 5-wood 220 yards, and don't factor in wind, elevation, and lie. A pro like Tiger Woods knows that, under certain conditions, a club he usually hits 220 yards may go 260, but in other situations he may only be able to hit it 180. You need to think this way, too.

Okay, so your downwind, downhill 5-wood tee shot effectively gives you 245 yards. With the wind at your back, the tendency is for the wind to straighten out any draw or fade, so your chances of hitting the fairway are good. This would leave you a nice little 120-yard shot to the pin.

But what if you're teeing off against the wind or, most commonly on this hole, with a crosswind from left to right? Into the wind, your 5-wood would go 20 yards shorter than normal. Even if you hit it in the fairway—which will now be more difficult since a high-flying 5-wood will hook or slice more into the breeze—you would then face a 155-yard iron into the wind. So, into the wind, your tee shot should be either a 3-wood or a driver. If you're confident that you can hit a low, controlled shot with a driver, this is the perfect place for it; if not, then I recommend that you play a 3-wood. If you can normally hit your 3-wood 235 yards, the effect of the headwind versus the elevated tee will nearly cancel each other out, so a well-played shot will leave you about 130 yards in. One more thing: If your choice is a 3-wood, make a controlled, balanced swinging action. If you think you have to kill the ball to reach an ideal landing spot, you're better off using the driver.

Here's a tip that will help you on driving holes where you need accuracy: Play your 3-wood without using a tee. Instead, play the shot "off the deck." Since you can roll the ball anywhere you want on the teeing ground, take advantage by giving yourself a slightly puffy lie. It's actually to your advantage, when hitting a 3-wood into the wind, to have just a little grass behind the ball. That little bit of grass will get between the ball and the clubface, and the result is what the pros call a "shooter" or "flyer." The ball takes off like a rocket with very little spin and on a shallow trajectory so you get some extra roll.

You don't need to make any swing adjustments, other than to play the ball one to two inches back in your stance from where you'd normally play it for a teed-up driver.

If the wind is crossing on this hole as it often is, hitting the fairway becomes more difficult. The wise play is to hit a low shot that won't get blown away by the wind—a 2-iron, or whatever club you feel is most likely to keep the ball low and straight. You may be sacrificing some distance, but you'll have a much better chance of hitting the green from the fairway, even from farther back, than you will from the rough.

(*A note to the B and C players:* I've gone into great detail discussing how to manage the tee shot here, particularly because on this elevated tee, wind is a prime factor. I won't repeat all this information in your sections, however; the same basic principles I've described for the A player will apply to you as well.)

That said, let's get back to your hole strategy. On most days, a good tee shot will leave you with an approach shot of somewhere between 110 and 140 yards—likely a wedge, 9-, or 8-iron. Now don't start licking your chops just yet. Even though you've got a short iron in hand, remember that this green usually does not hold approach shots well. And you don't want to hit your approach left of the green or over it. So wherever the pin is located, plan on landing the ball a bit short of it. This way, if the ball releases (rolls forward), you might wind up "stiff," but if it checks up you'll still have a reasonable putt at a birdie.

An additional thought on the approach from the fairway: Remember that the green is relatively small. If the pin is tucked either left or right, shade your shot a little toward the center. If you hit the dead center of this green every time with your approach here, you'll always have a reasonable birdie putt.

If your tee shot finds the rough, you have to play even more cautiously. Since you probably will be hitting a well-lofted club, getting the ball up and out of the rough should not be a big problem. However, keeping the shot under control might be, since the ball is going to release more than usual. You may want to land the ball a few yards short of the green and plan on it bounding and rolling perhaps 30 to 40 feet toward the hole. Finally, always aim your approach shot from the rough toward the center of the green, since you won't have the same control of your direction as when you're hitting from the fairway.

Once you've reached the green, you'll see that, as at most holes at Shinnecock, there are no abrupt slopes in the greens. However, you'll find any number of small, subtle breaks. That's one of the great things about many of the old, classic courses: You really have to give your putt a good read no matter what the angle, because every putt will break just a little bit differently.

A perfect read on your 15- to 20-footer may net you a birdie, but don't be disappointed with two putts and par 4 on the innocent-looking 1st hole at Shinnecock Hills.

Player A is so pumped up and confident that he has one thing in mind: attacking the hole and scoring birdie. With the wind at his back, he ignores my advice and pulls out the driver. I can see from where he is aiming that he plans to carry the right corner of the dogleg; his intention is to hit a powerful draw shot that bends back to the center of the fairway and leaves him a short wedge into the pin which is cut in the right center portion of the green. I know already that when Player A completes this hole he will have learned the difference between smart and stupid strategic thinking.

Instead of swinging at a speed that allows him to stay balanced, he comes "out of his shoes," meaning that he gives it all he has. As a result, he leaves too much weight on his right foot and leg on the downswing rather than making a solid shift into his left side. This fault causes him to "fall back and fire," or hit the ball too much on the upswing. Player A is a strong player, so regardless of his fault the ball flies 240 yards, but unfortunately into a bad lie in the right rough.

From here, he plays a wedge back to the short fairway grass in front of the green. No matter what your handicap, this is the smartest shot to hit; being aggressive in this situation and trying to reach the green with a less lofted club will only compound your problems and lead to a bad score.

Player A is so rattled that, in trying to pitch the ball close to the hole with a sand wedge, he looks up before impact and hits the shot to the back of the green. Shook up further, and cursing himself for being stupid, he runs his first putt well by the hole. Fortunately, he makes a nice comeback putt for a score of 5.

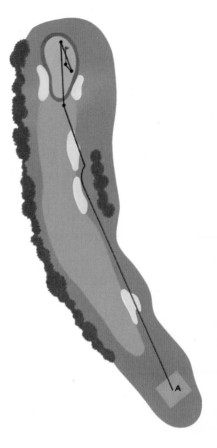

COMMON STRATEGIC AND SHOT-MAKING ERRORS BY THE A PLAYER

- Trying to cut too much off the corner with a driver tee shot
- Crying over spilled milk

Butch's Lessons

Play yourself into the round with a smart tee shot and a shot at par. This hole invites you to put the ball in play with a safe tee shot, and still have a short iron or wedge left. But Player A risked hitting into trouble just so he could have a "flip wedge" into the green. Don't let yourself make such silly mistakes. Play your tee shot as it was designed to be played, with a 3-wood or long iron up the center of the fairway. More important, make an on-balance swing.

Don't let one bad tee shot negatively influence the way you play the shots that follow. Play each hole one shot at a time, giving each your utmost confidence. If you make a mistake, accept it, then get on with the business at hand. The old saw, "what's done is done," is the mental attitude common to all top-notch golfers.

The B Player

For a 14-handicap player like you, the 1st at Shinnecock is an inviting opener, offering a good chance to start the round with a confidence-boosting par 4. Most B players will have no trouble with the distance. The key to the hole, again, is tee shot accuracy.

In order to hit the green in regulation, you need to be playing your second shot from the fairway. Again, the smart play is to hit the club from the tee that you feel you can hit accurately. Since the wind is with you, the most logical play is a lofted fairway wood from the tee.

It's always important to employ a balanced swing, but particularly on hole number 1 when you should be playing yourself into the round.
Notice how fully my weight has shifted over to my left foot and how comfortably erect my posture is. Follow this example.

The greater loft on a 3- or 5-wood as compared with the driver, along with the slightly shorter shaft, should make it just a little easier to make good contact on that first swing of the day. A useful tip for the 1st tee: Whatever club you choose, make a swing that feels like it's a little slower and a little more compact than normal.

You should aim for the left side of the fairway, avoiding any temptation to go near the bunkers or deep rough on the right. Let's say you go with a 3-wood and make nice solid contact with the ball. Including a boost of about 10 yards for the downhill tee shot, you're likely to be out there about 220 yards—on the short grass to boot.

Given this scenario, you're likely to have a shot of about 145 yards to the middle of the green. The green is fairly small so, even though you don't have a long shot, my advice would be to aim for the center of the green. Remember that if you're on the middle of this green, you're not likely to have a long putt no matter where the pin is located.

From 145 yards out, most B players will need a 6- or 7-iron. We already know that the green is not likely to hold your shot very well, so there's no sense in trying to boost an extra-high shot all the way to the flag. Instead, plan a slightly lower shot that will land around the front fringe and release to the middle of the green. You can do this by assuming your normal address position, except for two small adjustments: Choke down on the grip just a fraction of an inch, and play the ball about two inches back from its normal position, which is to say just about opposite the middle of your stance. This automatically puts your hands slightly more ahead of the clubface, delofting it by a degree or two to give you that slightly lower flight.

Again, make a swing that feels slow and compact, with the clubshaft traveling no farther back than to a three-quarter position. Try to play a shot that will land on the front fringe and then release gently toward the center of the green. You might surprise yourself and wind up with a good birdie putt.

Let's next take into consideration a very realistic possibility: Despite your best intentions, you put your tee ball in the rough. This is nothing to be dismayed about. No matter how positive you try to be about your tee shots, the fact is that most middle-handicap players will miss more fairways than they hit. Look, Tiger Woods, who is already one of the top players in the world, hits no more than 70 percent of the fairways with his drives. So it doesn't make much sense for you to be distraught when you miss one.

Let's say you pull your 3-wood into the left rough. Since the hole is playing a little longer with your off-line tee shot, you have 155 yards left. Ordinarily this would mean you'd need a 5- or 6-iron. However, if the ball is sitting reasonably well in the rough, you will actually get more distance on the shot, because the ball won't have as much backspin and will run more after it lands. Taking all this into consideration, I'd suggest you select a 7-iron. Aim the ball at the open right center of the green, trying to land the ball 10 to 15 yards short. If it comes out "hot," as it usually will, you'll get 20 yards of bounce and roll, putting the ball on the middle of the green.

Sometimes, though, you'll find that the ball doesn't come out of the rough quite like you planned. If it lands "soft," as it sometimes will, your ball will end up short of the green. However, this is a far better position than you'd be in by flying the ball onto the green and watching it bound way over. You'll be left with a chip of perhaps 60 to 90 feet, but you'll have an open run to the hole wherever it is located. On long chips such as this, select a low-lofted iron and play the ball in the right-center of a very narrow stance. Your hands should be slightly ahead of the ball. Because of the low loft, you'll need only a very brief, arms-dominated stroke both back and through to get the ball off and running. Even with a long iron, you can impart a sufficient amount of backspin on the ball to slow its speed. A good chip should leave you with a very makable par putt. Too often, I see a B player putting from long distance, and wasting a stroke because he or she knocks the ball well past the hole.

Don't overread this putt—if you see little or no break, keep the ball inside the hole and stroke firmly. Keep your head still and listen for the putt to drop.

Player B smartly selects a 3-wood to tee off with, and he even remembers to aim left to avoid severe trouble on the opposite side of the fairway, and to allow for his left-to-right fade. Ironically, however, he swings the club on such a perfect inside-square-inside path, and with such smooth tempo and rhythm, that he hits the ball dead straight. The ball never fades, leaving him a "flyer" lie in the rough, a 5-iron's distance to the green.

Player B intelligently allows for the ball flying farther than normal, but gears down too much, choosing a 7-iron. Consequently, even though he makes a good swing, the ball falls well short of the green on the right side.

In playing a long chip with a low iron, it's critical that you set your hands ahead of the ball at address (*left*), and control the downswing with your arms (*right*).

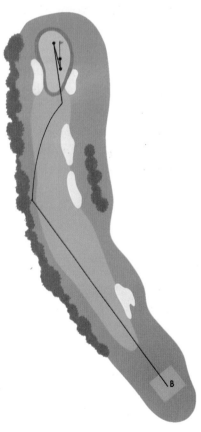

Remembering the advice I gave him on the long-iron chip, Player B hits a shot to within 3 feet of the cup. However, he sort of just gently coaxes the ball with his next stroke, leaving it short of the cup, on the low side. He putts the ball in for a score of 5.

COMMON STRATEGIC AND SHOT-MAKING ERRORS BY THE B PLAYER

- Not choosing the right club
- Hitting weak short putts

Butch's Lessons

Reading "flyer" lies is an art that must be learned. The pros regularly practice hitting shots out of various lies in the rough, so that they know precisely how far the ball will travel with a particular club. Do the same, and you'll rarely pick the wrong club from the rough.

Many amateurs do not hit their short putts firmly enough. The softer you hit short putts, the more any break (as well as any imperfections in the greens) will affect them. If you are in doubt about how to play a putt from less than 5 feet, my advice is that, unless you see a noticeable break, you start the ball inside the hole and putt it firmly, so that you take out most if not all of the break. That's what A players do.

The C Player

This is also an inviting opening hole for you, because it is reachable with two good shots. Since you hit a normal drive about 210 yards, and taking into account that the tee shot is downhill, you're likely to have no more than 150 yards for your second shot—perhaps a 4- or 5-iron.

I'd still recommend that you play a 3-wood here, however. I realize that this may make it tougher for you to reach the green in two—and, despite my advice to both Player A and Player B to play this hole conservatively, I do want you to get on in two and make a par or birdie. I couldn't blame you if you decided to try the driver from this tee. I would, however, caution you about the bunkers to the right, and note that the prevailing wind is in that direction, and also remind you that most of your "misses" slice to the right. I'd therefore ask you to align your stance and clubface to start the ball at the left edge of the fairway.

Player C aims correctly down the left side of the fairway, but cuts across the ball drastically. The ball starts down the middle, but starts sliding right and catches that first bunker at the corner of the dogleg. Not a terrible shot, but one that could have been avoided— or at least improved upon—had Player C arrived at the course early enough to go through proper stretching and practice routines.

As tends to happen on great courses such as Shinnecock, a little mistake costs you. What now? You're about 160 yards from the green, in the middle of the bunker with a fair lie. This bunker has a lip that you must get over, although it's not too high. Maybe you can hit a 7-wood over the lip, over another bunker on the right side 50 yards from the green, and onto the green in two?

My advice? Don't even try it.

My reasons? Several. First, you have to catch this ball perfectly off the sand with your lofted wood to get it over the lip in front of you. If you hit the ball thin, you might bury it under the lip, and your first hole can turn into a nightmare. And, let's face it, if you hit every shot the way you wanted to, you wouldn't be a high-handicapper. Second, say you get it out over the lip but hit the ball "fat," so that it doesn't carry to the green; you might easily catch that fairway bunker farther up, and leave yourself a super-tough long bunker third shot.

My advice is that you take a lofted iron, perhaps a 7 or 8, and plan to hit a controlled shot of about 100 yards to the middle of the fairway. Don't try for the macho shot all the way to the green. Assume a slightly open stance, with the ball at the midway point between your feet, and dig your feet slightly into the sand. A key to good fairway bunker recoveries is to stay very "quiet" with your lower body and to control the swing with your arms. Remember, you don't have to swing hard here. Your goal is to contact the ball first and hit a simple shot of around 100 yards into the fairway.

Player C decides against playing the low-risk shot, and hits the 7-wood instead. However, because he hits the ball a little heavy and off line, it falls well short of the hole, in the back of the left bunker. Now, he faces a downhill lie.

Don't make the same mistake as Player C did from the fairway bunker. Hit a controlled shot with a lofted iron, making sure to keep your lower body relatively quiet and swing the club with your arms.

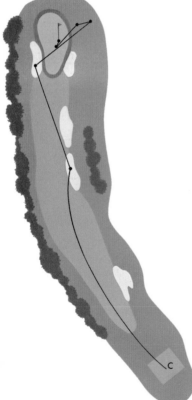

Instead of opening the clubface and hitting well behind the ball, he sets the blade square to the target and makes clean contact with the ball. The ball shoots over the green into deep rough.

He takes three shots to get down, scoring double-bogey 6.

COMMON STRATEGIC AND SHOTMAKING ERRORS BY THE C PLAYER

- Getting to the course late; not warming up correctly
- Slicing the driver from the tee
- Gambling on recoveries from trouble

Butch's Lessons

You played this hole with your heart. But low-handicap golfers play with their head.

The most important strategic mistake you made was arriving later than planned. Ideally, you want to arrive at the course early enough to be able to devote 30 minutes to a warm-up session. Start out by doing some simple stretching exercises, such as toe-touches and side-bends, just to get the blood flowing.

Hit about a dozen soft wedge shots, to further loosen the muscles and get a feel for the club making contact with the ball. Next, hit a few midirons and fairway woods before moving to the driver. Only hit about a half-dozen drives, paying close attention to the ball's shot patterns. If the ball is slicing, there are a few simple adjustments you can make in an attempt to correct the faulty flight path: assume a stronger grip; take the club further inside; make a more rounded shoulder turn. Next, hit about three more wedge shots to lock in a smooth tempo.

Ideally, you should also hit a couple of bunker shots, to familiarize yourself with the sand's texture. Then hit a few chips, so you can get used to that technique; it's one you'll probably be using right from the get-go. Last, hit a couple of short and long putts to test the green's speed and enhance your distance control.

This may sound like a lot of work, but it will be well worth your time. Ben Hogan used to purposely drive his car slowly to the course; then upon arriving in the locker room, he tied his shoes extra slowly, just to put himself into a more relaxed mode. Of course, he also gave himself plenty of time to warm up. Players on all levels should follow his example.

Now, let's talk technique.

If you could eliminate that slice with your driver, the game would be a lot easier. A prime cause of the slice is one you can't see—a grip that's too tight on the club. When you grip tightly, your tendency is to pull the club across the target line. Too much grip tension also guarantees that even if the rest of your swing is sound, you'll leave the clubface open at impact. So, hold the club as lightly as you can throughout the swing. I guarantee that no matter how light it feels, you won't let go of the club. Keep your grip tension-free and let the club fly through the impact zone, and your shots will fly longer and straighter.

DRILL (FOR GROOVING A LIGHT GRIP)

Sometimes it's difficult to figure out just how firmly you're holding the club. Therefore, with the help of a friend, test your grip pressure.

In practice, after hitting a few shots with different clubs, have your friend gently pull a club out of your hands. If you're gripping correctly, you should feel just a little resistance in your hands as the club is pulled out. If your friend has to forcefully tug the club out of your hands, and you feel yourself holding on, you know you need to lighten your grip.

Here's another way to think about it: If a rating of 1 is how you would hold a soap bubble, and a 10 is how you'd hold a rope in a tug-of-war, then the right grip pressure is probably around a 6 or 7 for most full shots.

Bringing these images to the golf course will help you grip the club with the correct amount of pressure.

Too many high-handicappers take unreasonable gambles from fairway bunkers, especially considering the fact that their contact with the ball is less consistent than that of good players. Never try a recovery shot from sand, trees, or deep rough without thinking about it carefully beforehand. Do you honestly think you can play the shot successfully at least seven times out of ten? If not, look for an alternate recovery shot that you know you can make. Your overall score will be better for it.

HOLE	1	2	3	4	5	6	7	8	9	OUT	
YARDS	366	380	485	177	368	373	103	515	356	3123	
PAR	4	4	5	3	4	4	3	5	4	36	
Player A	5										
Player B	5										
Player C	6										
HOLE	10	11	12	13	14	15	16	17	18	IN	TOTAL
YARDS	183	508	121	339	339	417	407	452	510	3276	6399
PAR	3	5	3	4	4	4	4	4	5	36	72
Player A											
Player B											
Player C											

Perched on the inland side of a rising slope separating San Francisco's Lake Merced from the Pacific Ocean is Olympic, a course with the nickname Giant Killer, because it has a reputation for beating up the game's greatest golfers.

Measuring 6715 yards from the back tees, and being much shorter from the men's middle tees, Olympic is the shortest course among the active U.S. Open sites that include such monsters as Winged Foot West in New York and Congressional in Maryland. Yet this championship course has no Napoleon complex; in fact, many pros rate it the toughest venue of all.

Off the tee, you are constantly hitting through chutes of eucalyptus, cypress and cedar trees, and tall pines. As if that's not intimidating enough, the fairways are super narrow, and bordered by thick Italian ryegrass rough that forces you to hit a recovery shot with a high-lofted iron, or with a wedge. Postage stamp greens surrounded by yawning bunkers make the golfing experience even more difficult. Add to that an eerie damp fog that rolls in often off the Pacific, and you'll understand why sportswriter Jim Murray said this about Olympic: "This is not a golf course, it's a 6700-yard haunted house. If it were human, it'd be Bela Lugosi. I think it turns into a bat at midnight. It's Public Enemy Number One, Al Capone, John Wilkes Booth."

It's no wonder that, in the three U.S. Opens hosted by Olympic, only four men have broken par for 72 holes. What's more, each time, one of golf's great champions collapsed—first Ben Hogan, then Arnold Palmer, then Tom Watson. Before arriving at Olympic, this trio of pros had won a total of 24 major championships. Collectively, after leaving Olympic, they never won another.

The first time the Open was held at Olympic was in 1955, when Jack Fleck upset Hogan. During the first three rounds, the ever-accurate Hogan played a 3-wood off the 18th tee for position. On day four, he chose a driver. That proved to be a big mistake. He hooked the ball into the deep rough, then took three shots to get out. Hogan lost the lead, but luckily tied Fleck. However, he was so upset by his mental error on the last hole of the Championship that he lost the next day's playoff.

In the 1966 Open at Olympic, Palmer led by seven strokes midway through the fourth round, but collapsed on the back nine, shooting a "Jack Benny" score of 39. He too managed to get himself into a playoff with Billy Casper; he, too, lost.

In the 1987 Open, third-round leader Tom Watson never recovered from his shaky Sunday start of three bogeys in the first five holes. He lost to Scott Simpson.

The man most responsible for making Olympic more difficult than it was when Willie Watson originally designed it in 1924 is course designer Robert Trent Jones. Jones tweaked the Lake Course by shrinking the fairways down to 25 yards in the landing areas and making the rough much more punishing.

There is no doubt that Olympic is the ultimate thinking man's course. You can't just take out your driver on the par-4 and par-5 holes without thinking out a sensible strategy. You can't always attack the flags on approach shots. You can't always charge putts on the small, slippery greens.

You may never get a chance to set foot on Olympic. Still, it would be smart for you to learn how to play one of these short, narrow par-4 holes, since the high cost of real estate means that many of today's courses are shorter and laid out in a fashion similar to this San Francisco masterpiece.

Of all the par-4 holes at Olympic, the 2nd, at a mere 380 yards from the middle tees, is recognized as the most brutal. Writing about Olympic in *Grand Slam Golf*, *Golf* magazine's editor-in-chief George Peper writes:

After a benign opening hole, it's down to business at the 2nd hole, where the "swoop factor" comes sharply into play. Virtually every hole at Olympic owes some aspect of its challenge to the fact that the terrain swoops from the seaside sandhills down toward the west shore of Lake Merced. The 2nd hole plays across the side of that hill, with the terrain pitching the ball from right to left. At the same time, the hole moves slightly against the hill toward a plateau green offset to the right. The genius of this hole is that visually it does not engender comfort, either from the tee or on the approach.

Another element that makes this hole so difficult is the dew-covered fairway. This may surprise you, but the fairway surfaces at Olympic are almost always wet. No matter what handicap you play to, you must understand how this element of nature comes into play.

The A Player

Your thinking—to lay up short of the upslope—was good, but frankly that 2-iron you just hit so nicely down the middle of the fairway is not the best club for the job at hand. I know by the look on your face that this surprises you, but when you realize how hitting into an upslope kills distance, and how lucky you were that the ball trickled back down to a flat spot on the fairway, you'll see I'm right.

That powerful 205-yard 2-iron shot you hit sat down practically in its own ball mark on the dew-covered uphill slope, costing you about 20 yards of roll. What's more, had the ball come to rest on the slope, you would be facing an extremely difficult uphill shot from 170 yards. As it turns out, you're still too close to the slope for comfort; hitting a shot with a hill close in front of you makes the approach much more intimidating, and difficult.

Don't flirt with the slope. Next time, hit a 3-iron to ensure that you land the ball on a level area of fairway, and about ten yards short of the slope, even if it means playing a slightly longer approach into the green. Only hit the 2-iron if there's a strong wind at your back and you can eat up much of the slope with it. Similarly, if you feel confident about your swing, blow the ball over the severest part of the upslope with a wood.

Enough lectures. Play away.

In analyzing his approach of approximately 175 yards, the A Player should realize that, due to the wet fairway, moisture will inevitably come between the ball and the clubface at impact. As a result, the grooves on the clubface will not be able to grab hold of the ball and impart backspin on the shot, so the ball will fly around 10 yards farther than normal. Therefore, if you normally hit a 5-iron from 175 yards, you should hit a 6-iron now. Also, because the pin is cut on the right center of the putting surface, the smart play is to hit the shot to the open area, or "fat," of the green, left of the hole.

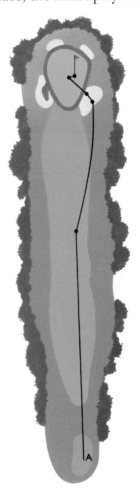

Watching intently, I see that Player A correctly chooses the 6-iron to allow for the "flyer." However, instead of aiming at an area left of the flag and hitting a straight shot, he plays a draw. Attempting to attack the flag, he tries to fly the ball from right to left, over the trap to the right of the green. The shot fails to curve, because the same dampness reduces sidespin.

Now, in the trap, with very little green between the lip of the bunker and pin, he tries to finesse the ball out. The ball never gets out of the sand. Fortunately he hits his next bunker shot stiff to the hole, for a tap-in bogey.

COMMON STRATEGIC AND SHOT-MAKING ERRORS BY THE A PLAYER

- Failing to consider all course conditions
- Using the wrong technique in sand

Butch's Lessons

As good a player as you are, you'll never reach the next level of becoming a scratch player if you don't take the time and care to weigh all the conditions. When it came to judging wind direction, the heaviness of air, the speed of the fairways and greens—even the effects of dew—Jack Nicklaus and Ben Hogan were the best. Take a lesson out of their book if you want to shoot par scores. There's no secret to accomplishing this goal; simply give yourself more time to think strategic thoughts, as well as swing thoughts.

You were right to try to finesse the ball from sand. The lie was level and the ball was sitting up. Besides, you have the feel and talent to hit the ball close from here. Here's how to hit that short shot over a high lip: Play the ball up in your stance, open the clubface a little more than usual for a bunker shot, make your left-hand grip a little weaker (Ken Venturi recommends playing this shot with a strong grip and a full follow-through, but I don't agree), cock the club up steeply on the backswing, and *slap* the sand with your right hand on the downswing, taking very little follow-through. The ball will pop right up, landing softly just over the lip and on the green.

Assuming a weaker grip and taking very little follow-through will allow you to cock the club up steeply on the backswing and slap the sand on the downswing, popping the ball up and landing it softly on the green.

The B Player

Well-played tee shot! I would rather have seen you hit your 3-wood here, instead of your driver, simply because its added loft makes it easier to control. But I like very much the way you handled the driver. You were very careful to set up correctly, you employed a smooth practice swing that was an exact rehearsal of the swing you intended to put on the ball, and you picked an interim spot between the ball and target. You also played your left-to-right fade shot, although I must admit that you flirted with the trees bordering the left side of the fairway. Next time, I suggest you tee up on the right side of the teeing area, to give your shot more room. Still, you hit an exceptionally long drive, 230 yards down the fairway. Let's see what you do from 150 yards.

Since Player B is a bogey golfer, he should be calculating in his head how he is going to ensure a score of 5, while still giving himself a chance at par. The smart play is for him to take the normal club (the hill and the flyer offsetting each other) and let his fade work the ball from the left side of the green toward the pin. (Isn't it interesting that the smart golfer, who takes all these factors into account, and the dumb one, who just hears a distance and reaches into his bag, will end up using the same club for this shot? Sometimes this game is easier than it looks.)

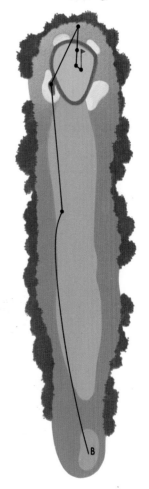

Player B does not follow the same strategy that I mapped out for him in my head. He chooses the correct club, a 5-iron, but rather than swinging smoothly, he goes after the shot. Maybe, in his subconscious mind, he thought he was going to come up short. Whatever the reason, because he swings too fast, he comes over the top and pulls the shot into an island of rough grass in the sand trap left of the green. More and more modern courses feature these hazardous areas in bunkers, so be prepared.

Player B proves to me that he had never before run into this type of greenside shot. He assumes a closed stance, closes the clubface of a 60-degree wedge, then pulls the club down hard into the back of the ball. The shot flies over the back of the green, where he leaves himself a tough up and down. Not surprisingly, he chips poorly, then two-putts for a double-bogey 6.

COMMON STRATEGIC AND SHOTMAKING ERRORS BY THE B PLAYER

- "Pressing" an iron shot
- Using the wrong greenside technique

Butch's Lessons

Any time you try to put more oomph behind an iron shot, the natural tendency is to hit a pull. If you select a weaker club for the distance at hand, swing it smoothly and confidently. Don't doubt yourself; negative thinking always leads to problems.

DRILL (FOR SLOWING DOWN YOUR SWING SPEED ON IRON SHOTS)

Hit shots off a low tee, with a variety of irons, for about an hour.
On the course, pretend the tee is there, and you'll be more apt to swing smoothly, make square contact at impact, and hit the ball accurately.

In playing a short shot off the cushioned grass with a sand wedge, employ this technique:

Take an open stance.

Open the clubface wide and set it down behind the ball.

Swing the club back on an upright arc, exaggerating the hinging action of your wrists.

An open stance and open clubface are two essential keys to playing a soft-landing short shot out of cushioned greenside rough.

Swing down, hitting a spot just behind the ball. This will allow you to loft the ball high, and once it hits the green it will roll gently toward the hole.

The C Player

Whereas the B player can allow for a fade, Player C must allow for a slice. The trouble is, on a narrow hole such as this, I fear the C player will aim too far left. Let's see how he approaches the tee ball.

Well, I hate to say it, but I guessed it. Not only does he aim too far left, he exaggerates the open stance, and plays the ball too far forward. No surprise then that the ball sails high into the air, follows a severe slice pattern, and finishes in the right rough.

He smartly lays up with a 9-iron, and puts the ball smack dead in the middle of the fairway.

Now some 100 yards from the hole, he plays another 9-iron shot that lands 15 feet from the cup.

Excited, he calms himself by looking at the break from behind the ball, from behind the cup, and from both sides of the ball-hole line. He takes two nice practice strokes, steadies his body over the ball, and uses a pendulumlike arms-shoulders stroke. The ball drops in. Par!

The reason the C player is able to score so well on such a difficult hole is that, following a poor drive, he kept his

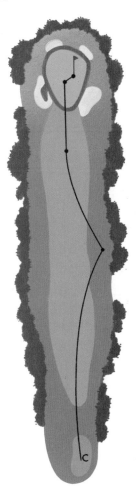

head and played strategically smart golf. Once on the green, he never let his elation take over. He concentrated on the task at hand; figuring the break in the green and making a smooth stroke. The par is well deserved.

COMMON STRATEGIC AND SHOTMAKING ERRORS BY THE C PLAYER

- Not knowing the art of playing the percentages (off the tee)
- Not adopting good setup fundamentals

Butch's Lessons

It seems silly that I would be giving you a couple of lessons after you just scored par. But if you're really serious about wanting to bring your game to another level, you'll have to make some changes.

First of all, on the tee shot, you would have given yourself a much better chance of hitting the fairway if you had adopted a square setup position, aimed straight down the left side, and let the ball fade back into play.

Sooner or later, slicers must face reality: A square setup will promote more controlled shots.

The next time you hit practice balls, I want you to set your feet, knees, hips, and shoulders parallel to the target line. Position the ball opposite your left heel, or slightly behind it as do many of the pros.

Work on this address position until you see improvement in your ball-striking ability. That slice of yours is costing you vital distance off the tee. Without it, you could pick up as much as 40 yards. On approach shots, you will then hit more lofted clubs, and hit more greens in regulation as a result.

This practice assignment may sound like hard work, but if you sacrifice some playing time and work extra hard, you will start scoring better and enjoying the game even more than you do already.

DRILL (FOR GROOVING A SQUARE SETUP)

Lay one club down behind the ball, along the target line. Set a second club down parallel to the target line, then set your feet square to it—toes touching the clubshaft.

Hitting shots in this practice station is something even the pros do to help them groove a square setup position.

HOLE	1	2	3	4	5	6	7	8	9	OUT	
YARDS	366	380	485	177	368	373	103	515	356	3123	
PAR	4	4	5	3	4	4	3	5	4	36	
Player A	5	5									
Player B	5	6									
Player C	6	4									
HOLE	10	11	12	13	14	15	16	17	18	IN	TOTAL
YARDS	183	508	121	339	339	417	407	452	510	3276	6399
PAR	3	5	3	4	4	4	4	4	5	36	72
Player A											
Player B											
Player C											

MEDALIST GOLF CLUB
Par 5: 485 yards

Not far from Palm Beach, Florida, in the quiet town of Hobe Sound, sits the Medalist course, designed by Greg Norman and Pete Dye.

If you know course architecture, you know that Dye courses are anything but ordinary. If you know Greg Norman, you know he has a passion for hitting the ball prodigious distances in the air and gambling on approach shots. It should come as no surprise then that the end result of their collaboration is a 7179-yard championship course, one that requires golfers to hit their tee shots over huge expanses of water and wasteland and their approaches to an area on the green the size of a bath towel in order to keep the ball close to the hole. What makes the course even more challenging is that many greens are perched high above the fairway, making it extremely difficult to chip the ball close from the very tightly mowed sloping fringe or to save par from the deep greenside bunkers. The fairways are very tightly mowed too, making wood shots and pitches more testy; with no cushion underneath, it's easy to top a wood or skull a pitch. The good news: These surfaces, much like Astroturf baseball fields, cause the ball to run more, giving players more distance off the tee.

Still, I consider the course fair. That's because Norman and Dye offer alternative "back" and "member" tees that shorten the course considerably. From the back tees, the course measures 6564 yards; from the member tees, 5802 yards.

When you hit from either of these tees, the course is much more easily playable, although you'll still need all the clubs in your bag over 18 holes. You'll also have to remain very patient and think your way around, or else this layout will eat your lunch.

Ironically, one of the most challenging holes is the short par-5 third, measuring only 485 yards from the member tees, where I want you to imagine you're playing today. This hole is a relatively sharp dogleg right, requiring a carry of around 180 yards off the tee to clear a marshy area and reach the fairway. There is a long sand trap running down the right side of the fairway, so the ideal landing spot is down the left side. Hitting the ball to that target will allow you to get a bird's-eye view of the green, which seems as far away as the planet Pluto.

The priority on your second shot is not so much distance as it is accuracy. If your shot strays from the fairway, you'll find the ball amongst trees, on sand, atop pine needles, or in scrubby rough. The third shot is made more difficult by the plateau green, with a bunker left and right of it. The green is relatively small, too, so your approach shot demands precise club selection and pinpoint accuracy. The surface of the green looks flat, but because it's actually subtly crowned, most of the putts you'll face will have some small break.

Let's play it.

The A Player

I noticed that you set up for a power-fade shot, pointing your feet slightly left of target and aiming the clubface at a spot in the center of the fairway where you wanted the ball to finish. You got set, then looked back from the ball to target a few times. That's a good habit; that kind of intense focus on the target area raises a player's level of confidence and sends a positive message to the brain. Once the brain knows where you want to hit the ball, the body finds a way to swing the club correctly, according to the swing you rehearsed a couple of times before setting up to the shot. You B and C players can learn some good lessons about the importance of playing a video in your head before you swing, by watching how the A player focuses hard on the target. This preswing procedure also discourages you from looking at trees, fairway bunkers, and other trouble spots. Consequently, you're less apt to steer the ball away from trouble on one side of the fairway and hit it in a water hazard, for example, on the other side.

Your commitment to the shot was excellent, too. You swung the club nicely to the top, accelerated your lower body through impact, and flowed into a full finish.

Player A's drive lands 250 yards down the fairway, leaving him 235 yards to the green. The lie is level. Only a strong player who hits the ball long and high should try to hit this green in two. In this case, I think the smart play is to lay up with a long iron.

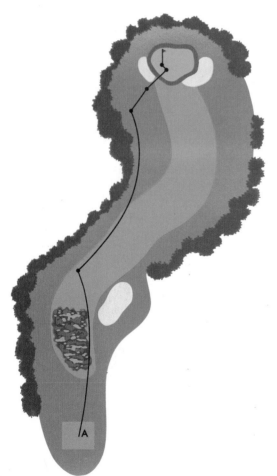

The machismo factor prompts the A player to take out his 3-wood, heedless of the trouble bordering the fairway. He wants to ensure birdie by hitting the green in two. The problem is, he must hit the perfect shot to reach—and hold—the green. If he should waver left or right, and land in a sandy spot or behind a tree, bogey comes into the picture.

Sure enough, in trying to hit the ball more powerfully, he hooks it into a sandy spot in the left rough, on those pine needles I spoke about. Now, instead of facing a fairly short pitch, he is confronted with a very tough lie from 35 yards, and a bad angle to the pin.

He fluffs his third shot. Next, he plays a nice pitch and run. The ball pitches short of the green and runs up the bank, landing just five feet from the hole. He converts the par putt. A decent result, despite the mental error he made playing his second shot, and the poor recovery shot he hit from pine needles. Score: par 5.

COMMON STRATEGIC AND SHOTMAKING ERRORS BY THE A PLAYER

- Not hitting a long-iron lay-up shot, with draw flight
- Not knowing how to hit a basic trouble shot

Butch's Lessons

One secret to scoring is knowing when to lay up and when to go for the green. Senior PGA Tour player Johnny Miller calls these *red light* and *green light* situations. *Go* on the green, *stop* on red. The fact that you had to hit your 3-wood on the screws to reach the green in two should have been enough to caution you not to try to

get home. Aside from that, the green itself is small and on a plateau, so nearly impossible to hold. Additionally, the penalties for not reaching the green are severe, as you discovered.

In this situation, you would have been much better off playing a draw with either a 4- or 5-iron. Either of these clubs will send the ball flying far down the fairway. All you have to do in order to impart some overspin on the ball is increase the rotation of your forearms and

When looking for added overspin and distance on a lay-up shot, increase the rotation of your forearms and hands through impact.

hands through impact, so that the toe of the club leads the heel and the clubface closes slightly at impact. This is an excellent shot to hit when you're looking for extra yards and don't have to hold a green. You normally hit the ball around 175 yards with the 5-iron; if you put overspin on the shot, you'll pick up about another 30 yards, owing to the fact that the fairways at the Medalist are fast-running. That's 205 yards! Add that to your 250-yard drive and you're left with a shot of 30 yards into the green, from the middle of the fairway. With a pitch and a putt you could score birdie.

I don't have to remind you that you landed on pine needles and messed that shot up, too. You tried to blast the shot out by digging the club deeper into the sand; the secret is to pick it cleanly. Here's how to recover:

First, realize that pine needles are loosely knitted together, so the slightest touch can dislodge the ball. You don't want to incur a penalty, so I suggest you start by holding the clubhead above the needles, just behind the ball. Play the ball just short of the midpoint in your stance, with your hands slightly ahead of the clubhead and a tad more weight on your left foot. Swing the hands back to level with your hips, keeping your wrists quiet. If you get too handsy and exaggerate the hinging of your wrists, you'll swing on an overly steep plane and hit the ball fat, just like you did.

The B Player

Player B moves the ball so far back in his stance that he blocks his tee shot out to the right, with the ball luckily just clearing the hazard. From there, he smartly hits a 5-iron, fading it from left to right so that it lands in the middle of the fairway, some 160 yards from the green. From there, he plays another 5-iron shot, but hits the ball off the toe. Luckily the ball lands on the bank of the front fringe, short of the right bunker. He chooses to putt from that spot. This is a smart play because the fringe grass at the Medalist is mowed down low. He just misses and taps in for a well-earned par.

COMMON STRATEGIC AND SHOTMAKING ERRORS BY THE B PLAYER

- Not setting up correctly to hit a drive with more carry
- Occasional toe hits with irons

Butch's Lessons

When you're looking to carry the ball farther than normal off the tee, there are a couple of adjustments to make. Move the ball up in your stance, playing it off your left instep. Then widen your stance, moving your right foot back about an inch or two (keeping it parallel to the target line—you don't want to close your stance here). Then take your normal swing.

The key to these adjustments is that this position will help you stay behind the ball a little longer, which is what gets the ball up into the air more, giving you the extra carry you want. And it lets you do it without

Playing the ball forward in your stance will promote a powerful upswing hit and more carry off the tee.

thinking too much about it, since trying too hard to stay behind the ball can cause you to open up and worsen your fade—or, worse, cause a reverse weight shift and a weak pop-up, the last thing you want.

The toe shot you hit with the 5-iron was caused by swinging out at the ball. I don't know who it was who brought "swing out" into the golf teacher's vocabulary. I do know that it's something my dad hated to hear, as do I. Rather than swing from in to out, the club should swing on an inside-square-inside path. To encourage this path, put a ball down on the grass. Lay a cardboard club box or a piece of PVC pipe about an inch outside the ball and parallel to the target line.

Address the ball and swing. You'll see that the secondary target line encourages you to release the hands, arms, and club in the hitting area. That action will allow you to work the club back to the inside. Before, there was no rotation in your arms. You simply extended both arms outward and stopped at impact. You must release.

The C Player

I can see by the look on Player C's face that he is petrified. Not only that, but once he sets up I can see he is not going to make a good swing and carry the hazard. His arms are outstretched too far, and very tense. Also, he is bending over in an exaggerated fashion. His backswing will be extra short and very steep. The releasing action of the arms-hands-club will be hindered greatly by excessive muscle tension.

Unfortunately, I am right. Player C's shot with the driver finds the hazard short of the fairway. He must re-tee the ball and play again, hitting three.

Re-teeing with a 3-wood, a club Player C has more confidence in, he seems to relax and makes a much more rhythmic swing. The ball carries the hazard and lands 180 yards down the right side of the fairway. Still, there's major room for improvement with regard to his setup. I'll discuss these changes shortly.

For his fourth shot, Player C hits a 5-wood down to a spot about 140 yards from the green.

Instead of making a smooth swing with a 5-iron, he pauses at the top, then pulls the club straight down into the turf. The result is a fat shot that leaves him 40 yards from the green.

The Medalist's 3rd hole features a plateau green, with devilish traps on both sides.

Facing the shot you see in the accompanying photograph, he tries to hit a delicate lofted pitch off the very tight fairway, which is not a high percentage shot for the bogey golfer. This time he hits the top half of the ball, running it over the green, some 50 feet from the hole. Fortunately, he two-putts, scoring triple-bogey.

COMMON STRATEGIC AND SHOTMAKING ERRORS
BY THE C PLAYER
- Bad posture at address
- Pausing too long at the top of the swing
- Playing a difficult, low-percentage soft pitch

Butch's Lessons
To promote the correct swing plane, bend from the ball-and-socket joints of your hips, never your waist. Stooping over encourages an overly steep plane. Relax your arms, too, so that they feel more like spaghetti and less like steel. Relaxed arms help you generate speed and power in the swing.

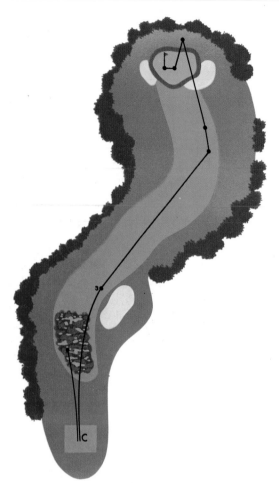

Don't consciously pause at the top of the swing. The pause should happen naturally as the club changes direction. Pausing disrupts the tempo of the swing and encourages you to pull the club down hard. To alleviate this problem, think of the swing as one continuous uninterrupted motion. Furthermore, concentrate on swinging into a full finish. The following drill will help you solve your problem.

DRILL (TO CURE LONG PAUSE PROBLEM AT THE TOP OF THE SWING)

When hitting shots on the practice tee, try to rotate your stomach or belt buckle toward the target as soon as you start your downswing.

If you practice this drill just every other day for about a week, when you get to the course, your shifting and rotating actions will kick in automatically the split second you reach the top. All of a sudden, your pause will be gone.

The next time you're 40 yards out, on a tight fairway, hitting to a green with an unguarded entranceway, and the pin is up front, don't think about playing a soft pitch. You told me yourself, before the round, that this is a shot you don't practice. So don't try it on the course until you've mastered it in practice. Instead, play a pitch and run. Here's what to do:

Play the ball back slightly in an open stance, so your hands are positioned ahead of the ball.

Keeping your lower body perfectly still, swing the club back so its shaft is parallel to the ground.

This is what you should look like, on the backswing, when playing a pitch-and-run shot.

This is what you should look like, on the downswing, when playing a pitch-and-run shot.

Allow your shoulders to rotate freely and your right wrist to hinge slightly.

On the downswing, rotate your right hip counterclockwise, and unhinge your right wrist, as these swing keys help you accelerate the club. Concentrate on keeping the club moving low through impact, so that you sweep the ball off the turf. The ball will fly relatively low, land in the fringe, bounce onto the green, then trickle to the hole.

HOLE	1	2	3	4	5	6	7	8	9	OUT	
YARDS	366	380	485	177	368	373	103	515	356	3123	
PAR	4	4	5	3	4	4	3	5	4	36	
Player A	5	5	5								
Player B	5	6	5								
Player C	6	4	8								

HOLE	10	11	12	13	14	15	16	17	18	IN	TOTAL
YARDS	183	508	121	339	339	417	407	452	510	3276	6399
PAR	3	5	3	4	4	4	4	4	5	36	72
Player A											
Player B											
Player C											

NATIONAL GOLF LINKS OF AMERICA
Par 3: 177 yards

In the sleepy town of Southampton, Long Island, a popular summer vacation spot for the wealthy, lies one of the game's gems: the National Golf Links of America. Located next door to the famous Shinnecock Hills, the "National," as it is most commonly called, is extra special. You know that the second you drive through the iron gates and down a winding road and suddenly come upon a grandiose Gatsby-like clubhouse that sits proudly atop a grassy hilltop and overlooks the Peconic Bay and the spectacular links-type layout completed by course architect Charles (C.B.) Macdonald in 1909.

A native of Chicago, Macdonald became smitten with the royal and ancient pastime in the 1870s while studying at St Andrews, Scotland's home of golf. This exceptional player and architect was one of those responsible for introducing golf to America. His list of creations include the Chicago Golf Club, Bermuda's Mid-Ocean, Yale in Connecticut, and Old White at the Greenbrier in West Virginia. No layout he designed, however, matches the quality of the National, considered by golf aficionados to be the first great course in America.

What makes National so special is that many of the holes are near duplicates of the most famous ones in Britain. The inspiration for this came when Macdonald read an opinion poll on the most popular holes conducted by England's *Golf Illustrated*, the world's first golf magazine.

Macdonald was a master researcher who truly believed that proper planning prevents poor performance. As for the construction of National, this is what William H. Davis said in the book, *Great Courses of the World:*

The actual construction of Macdonald's National Golf Links was not started until 1907, but it might be said that the preparatory work started much earlier.

Macdonald made two trips to Britain to study the most popular courses—St. Andrews, Prestwick, North Berwick, Hoylake, Sandwich, Deal, Westward Ho!, Machrihanish,

Littlestone, and Brancaster among them—and to collect sketches and surveyors' maps of the most highly esteemed holes.

After a period of exploration back home, he found the seaside land he wanted to build on. Not one to hurry himself, he took four years to complete the National, carefully utilizing the best natural features of the terrain and patiently reshaping the other stretches to fit the grand design: the creation of a course that would rank with the finest in the world.

Although Macdonald is considered one of the all-time truly ingenious course architects, the 250-acre parcel of land he built his masterpiece on made the job of cloning Britain's greatest links holes all that much easier. Honestly, if you blindfolded a Scot, then let him open his eyes and look out over the sprawling links, with its rolling terrain, tight fairways, pot bunkers, and small, speedy, undulating greens, he would certainly think he was playing golf in his homeland. There's gorse and long wavy grass, bayberry, huckleberry, blackberry bushes, and even a spot of heather here and there, just like on many of the overseas courses.

Under 7000 yards from the middle tees, National is not known for its length. It is a classic strategic design that rewards risk-takers who hit the correct shot and severely punishes those who fail. The winds blowing off the Atlantic Ocean from the south and Long Island Sound on the north make National a good test of golf for all calibers of player. Those who stray from the fairway or miss a green usually find themselves in one of the many sand bunkers spotted generously over the rolling land.

Local knowledge is an important link to scoring, because of the subtle breaks in the greens and the blind shots from the tee or fairway. So if you're a guest at the National, do the smart thing and hire a caddy who knows the course.

National has a good mix of par-3, par-4, and par-5 holes, and five are virtual imitations of the most celebrated holes in Britain: numbers 2, 3, 4, 7, and 13. The short par-4 2nd hole is modeled after the old 3rd at Royal St. George's. The 3rd, a rather strong par 4, presents the golfer with the same challenges he would be welcomed with at the Alps at Prestwick. The 4th is a clone of North Berwick's

Redan hole, which also features a tilted green angling downward from one side to the other. (This design feature has been copied often, most notably on the 7th hole at Shinnecock Hills, which is also named "Redan.") The 7th and 13th are modeled after two famous holes at St. Andrews, the Road Hole and the 11th at the Old Course, where the green lies on the lip of the river Eden.

The National is truly a blueblood private club that seeks no "press." It has hosted only one major event of national interest: the 1922 Walker Cup, a biennial match between the best amateur players of America and of Great Britain and Ireland. It does, nevertheless, have a guest policy, so you could be lucky enough to be invited there one day. If not, you should still know what it takes to play the 4th hole, because it is a classic style of hole that can be found in the work of several of today's top architects.

Known as the Redan, the 4th is a rather short par 3, measuring 177 yards from the middle tees. Yet, as is the case with most of National's holes, swirling wind and deep sand bunkers intimidate the mind as you stand on the tee looking at a long green that slopes severely from right to left. To fire a shot directly at a pin cut in the middle or left side of the putting surface, you must flirt with a yawning bunker located 12 yards in front of the green. A more cautious shot, played out to the right, must draw slightly in the air, or you'll land in another of four traps, or be left in the manicured fringe or on the far side of the green facing a long delicate downhill chip or putt.

Describing the Redan in *The Story of American Golf*, Herbert Warren Wind wrote:

On a strategic hole, the emphasis is on initiative. The player is given a choice of several routes to the green. On a one-shotter like the Redan, for example, he can generally get a 4 by steering away from the one serious hazard, a long harsh trap that follows the front edge of a raised green built on a traverse. The player who goes for the small untrapped opening to the corner of the green can get his par 3, but leaves himself a long putt and just about forfeits his chance for a possible birdie 2. The player who goes for the pin and gambles on carrying the trap before the green, or suffering the consequences if he plays his stroke inadequately, is rewarded for hitting the required shot with an easy 3 and a good chance for his 2.

The bottom line: The green is a small narrow target, surrounded by treacherous traps and trouble spots. Therefore, the smart strategy is to proceed with caution.

The A player must be able to judge the wind perfectly, pick the correct club for that "adjusted" distance to the hole, and not be drawn to a "sucker pin." Rather, he must honestly analyze his game, on that day, and know when and when not to attack the stick. Whether he or she is competing in a match- or stroke-play competition, the object is not to play stupidly and shoot an over-par score.

The B player should not play a weaker club than the A player, since this type of egotistical strategy leads to an overly long, speedy swing, and a mishit ball.

The priority of the C player is to take plenty of club and allow for his natural shape of shot. This is no hole to try a shot you aren't sure you can hit.

Now that I've given you a glimpse into the basic strategies involved in playing the Redan, let me walk you through the hole and discuss the finer points, so that when you play a hole like this you'll know the secrets to scoring.

The A Player

Because you're hitting to a small target surrounded by trouble, the priority of even a skilled player like you should be to hit the green, take two putts, and run to the next tee. Birdie is a bonus that usually comes on a rare calm day, when it's easier to judge distance, or if a long putt is made.

Since the wind frequently swirls from right to left, and virtually blows back into your face, pretend that is the situation today. Make believe, too, that the pin is cut in the right front center of the green. Play away.

Player A tosses grass up into the air, notes which way the flag is blowing, and looks at the tops of trees, to get a good read on the approximate strength and direction of the wind. Good: You determined that you were facing a "one-club wind," meaning in effect that you needed a less-lofted club than normal to make up for the 10 yards of distance you would lose. Since from 177 yards you normally play a 5-iron, you did right to choose a 4.

Because of the narrow green, however, I do not like your shot strategy. I can see from where you are aiming—at the right corner of the green—that you plan to play a right-to-left draw shot. You want the ball to land on the right front of the green and roll toward the pin; you feel that's the smartest shot to play when hitting into the wind. I think it's very dangerous, and not the percentage shot that a player of your caliber should choose to play. This is particularly true because you play your draw by aiming your club and body to the right, rotating your left hand and forearm in a clockwise direction on the backswing, then using the opposite hand-arm release

In setting up to play the 3-wood chip shot, play the ball in the middle of an open stance.

When playing the 3-wood chip shot, keep the wrists quiet on the backswing.

on the downswing—in other words, you play a draw using a "feel" method. This creates a lot of overspin, and with the shape of this hole there's a real danger that the ball will hit and run through the green into trouble. It's better to play your draw by aiming your body to the right (more or less depending on the degree of draw), setting the clubface down dead square to your target, then employing your normal swing. This method imparts less right-to-left overspin.

I would much rather see you simply hit the same 4-iron, but not get so cute with it. Play a straight shot instead, and let the wind hold the shot up. I'd also be more comfortable seeing you play a hard fade with the same club, or a soft cut with a 3-iron, even though this brings the front bunker into play. In all these cases, the ball will sit down much more quickly on the green.

Player A plays his draw anyway, hitting the ball exactly on the line he wants. However, because of the low loft of the club, and because he plays it back slightly in his stance to fight the wind, the ball flies lower. The low flight of the ball, plus the overspin he imparts on it, force it to race through the green into the second cut of heavy fringe. Now, instead of being faced with an easy two-putt situation, or even a makable birdie putt, he's confronted with a tricky chip.

To loft the ball over the fringe with a 3-wood, make a level, pendulum-type downswing action.

As good as you are with the wedge around the green, put it back in your bag; it's not the best club to use when your ball sits down in the second cut of fringe grass. No matter how much you've practiced hitting wedge shots around the green, from this lie, it's very difficult to judge how much air time and ground time to give the shot. In playing this shot with a pitching wedge, sand iron, or third wedge, using a pop-shot technique, players usually either: (1) employ an overly steep swing and hit an uncontrollable flyer, or (2) decelerate the club in the impact zone and leave the shot well short. For this reason, I want you to play a shot my dad taught me, and I've passed on to Tiger Woods, who's been making it famous: Hit it with a 3-wood!

The advantage of hitting this shot with a 3-wood is that it allows you to make a slower, shorter, level stroke that's easy to employ. Furthermore, the shape of the clubhead lets it slide through the grass and produce solid contact. In fact, I want you to feel like you're putting. Follow my directions, then try it yourself.

Position the ball in the middle of an open stance, with your hands in line with the clubface. Keep your wrists quiet, and control the stroke with your arms and shoulders (just like a putt), so the club stays level as it swings back and through.

See how easy it is; the 14 or 15 degrees of loft built into the club-face allow you to launch the ball softly over the fringe grass in front of you, so that it runs quietly to within 3 feet of the hole. Nice par putt conversion.

COMMON STRATEGIC AND SHOTMAKING ERRORS BY THE A PLAYER

- Hitting a fancy shot when the situation does not merit it
- Not having a full repertoire of short-game shots

Butch's Lessons

I'm not sure why, but many single-digit players seem to take par-3 holes for granted. What I mean is, when they come to these holes they sometimes lose respect for a par score. They try to gun the ball at the flag, most of the time hitting a fancy little draw or fade shot.

There is a time and a place to hit a creative shot. The situation has to be perfect. For example, if the green at National's Redan hole had been deeper and the pin back-left, the shot you played would have been perfect. I would have applauded you for hitting a draw. However, as you know, the pin was cut in the right front center of the green. Moreover, the green was as thin as a strip of breakfast bacon. There's no way you can hit a draw here at the National, or at any course with a similarly designed green.

Just for the heck of it, try to go back and think how many par-3 holes you bogeyed because you used this kind of faulty strategy. I'll bet the number is high.

The next time you play a hole designed like this, or any par-3 hole for that matter, concentrate harder on hitting the green. Only attack the flag by hitting a soft draw, low fade, or another fancy shot if the situation warrants it.

As to your short game, I'd like you to develop a wider range of shots. Granted, many of today's PGA pros play chips with either one of three wedges. However, they don't limit themselves to these clubs. Tiger Woods is probably the most creative chipper around. He uses anything from a wedge to a 3-wood. I suggest you go to your local practice green and hit chips from a variety of lies with a variety of clubs. That's what the pros do, and they learn new shots every day. In fact, that's how my father invented the 3-wood chip.

The B Player

In thinking about how you would handle this hole, I feared that you would pick a weaker club, then make a very aggressive swing. On the 2nd hole, you did that on your approach, and pulled the ball left of the green. This time you used your head. You chose a 5-wood and swung within yourself. Not letting your ego get in the way paid off. You made solid contact, the ball faded slightly from left to right, and landed on the green 25 feet from the hole.

You got a little too aggressive on your approach putt, and knocked it well by the hole. Just because a putt is uphill, and you face a birdie putt, don't think that's your signal to charge the hole. Just lengthen your stroke slightly, and maintain the same tempo. Remember, when you hit the ball too hard, you run the ball through the break, making it near impossible for it to fall into the cup. This mistake cost you a par, when you were so afraid of hitting your second putt too hard that you left it short. Don't let previous shots hinder what you do on the next shot. Concentrate on one putt at a time.

DRILL (FOR LEARNING TO PACE PUTTS)

To enhance your distance control on long putts, take your normal putting address and set the putterface squarely to a hole 25 feet away.

Next, turn your head and look at the hole. Keep your head in that same position and make a rhythmic stroke.

After a few hours of practice, you'll find that when you return to your normal setup you judge distance much better.

COMMON STRATEGIC AND SHOTMAKING ERRORS BY THE B PLAYER

- Letting the ego get in the way
- Getting greedy on the green

Butch's Lessons

I realize how easy it is to fall into the trap of trying to stay with your playing partners. You proved here that you can ignore the fact that the A player hit a more lofted club and can "play" your own shot. When you took the 5-wood out of the bag, you proved to me that you were starting to mature as a player. Ego is a tricky thing; my only advice is, if it bothers you that your playing partners hit irons when you must play woods, start practicing harder. But remember the old saying, "It's not how, it's how many."

As for that birdie putt, going for a 25-foot slider on a lightning-fast green is about as smart as crossing a city street against the light in midday traffic. Use common sense. Don't take unnecessary risks. You may make one out of 20 of these putts from 25 feet. I'll tell you the same thing I told the A player—and I tell Tiger Woods and Davis Love: Birdies are great, but sometimes you must respect par.

The C Player

You were smart to aim left and play for your slice. Unless you're "on" and hitting the ball accurately, you should always allow for your natural shape of shot. Your thinking was good, too; you knew that if the ball sliced too much, at least you would have a reasonable chance for a par, hitting your second shot from either the light fringe or the trap on the right. As it turned out, the ball ballooned in the air, and fell short in the bunker located left of the green.

The bunker shot you faced is exactly the kind of nightmare this hole design creates: a downhill lie, with the ball very close to the back lip, having to clear a high lip to a green sloping away from you. I hated to see you leave your second shot in the sand, but that resulted as much from a mental error as a physical one: trying to do too much with the shot. But your second attempt to get out of the bunker you played nicely out onto the green, and you made a good putt to save bogey.

COMMON STRATEGIC AND SHOT-MAKING ERRORS BY THE C PLAYER

- Hitting the ball too high
- Trying a pro-type sand shot

Butch's Lessons

The next time you're hitting a shot into the wind with a 5-wood, don't tee the ball up so high. I noticed that you had about half of the ball above the clubface, which is fine for a driver but not the 5-wood. Amateurs make this mistake all the time. The typical player worries so much about club selection that he or she forgets to analyze the situation. A good policy, particularly with a 5-wood, is to allow about a third of the ball to be atop the clubface. Incidentally, you don't want the top of the club to be level with the ball either. This low tee height could promote an overly steep backswing, and a sharp hit on the descent.

Let's discuss that mental error you made in the sand. Frustrated by what you thought was a good tee shot, you tried to hit a delicate sand shot just over the lip, and let it roll down to the hole. Frankly, these are not shots you should try, simply because you haven't practiced them. You paid the price for this mistake, leaving the ball in the bunker. You did, nevertheless, hit a good second sand shot, and concentrated hard and holed your putt for bogey, which is your "personal par" on a par 3.

When playing a 5-wood off a tee, a good policy is to allow about one-third of the ball to be atop the clubface.

The next time you land in a trap and face a slight downhill lie such as the one you had here, with the ball very close to the back lip, you should set your shoulders along the level of the slope, open the blade more, and swing down the slope a trifle harder than usual, making sure you hit the sand, not the ball.

HOLE	1	2	3	4	5	6	7	8	9	OUT	
YARDS	366	380	485	177	368	373	103	515	356	3123	
PAR	4	4	5	3	4	4	3	5	4	36	
Player A	5	5	5	3							
Player B	5	6	5	4							
Player C	6	4	8	4							
HOLE	10	11	12	13	14	15	16	17	18	IN	TOTAL
YARDS	183	508	121	339	339	417	407	452	510	3276	6399
PAR	3	5	3	4	4	4	4	4	5	36	72
Player A											
Player B											
Player C											

Hole 5
WINGED FOOT GOLF CLUB (EAST)
Par 4: 368 yards

The Winged Foot Golf Club, located in Mamaro-neck, New York, less than a half-hour from the Big Apple, is a place steeped in history. The West Course at Winged Foot has hosted the U.S. Open four times, and in 1997, the PGA Championship, the final major tournament of the season, was played there. Designed by A. W. Tillinghast, the West is known for its length, its narrow tree-lined fairways, but perhaps most of all for its well-guarded greens, which are creatively contoured and lightning fast.

It's a shame that, by comparison, the East Course at Winged Foot is so little known to the public, because it too is a terrific layout. I've always enjoyed playing the East Course much more then the West. It's a course with more character: more doglegs, smaller greens, and more interesting shots than its more famous brother, which just beats you up with its length (about 300 yards more than the East from the back tees). The West is a better course for a major championship, but for all but the very top professionals, the East Course is all the test anyone would ever need.

For our purposes, let's take a superb hole from this less-revered but classic layout. The 5th hole at Winged Foot East is a 368-yard par 4 when played from the men's regular markers. It is the ninth handicap hole on the course, so to a very good player it might be considered a birdie hole. Aptly named "Bootleg," this hole makes a sharp dogleg turn to the right. The hole's medium-width fairway runs slightly downhill between thick stands of trees; and farther to the right, out-of-bounds lurks. So, the tee shot must be played with precision. Players who opt to use a driver will have to hit it with a fade in order to keep from going through the fairway, since the turn in the dogleg is about 210 to 230 yards from this tee. There are no fairway bunkers, but at Winged Foot the rough is generally thick enough to make it very hard to control approach shots from it.

The green at hole 5 is smallish, and is well guarded by bunkers on the right and on the left. They are fairly deep, as are almost all Tillinghast bunkers, and getting up and down from them for a par is difficult. The green also presents a challenge as a hump runs across it from left to right, and at a slight angle as you approach the green, so putting can be tricky if you're not on the correct side. For our purposes here, let's say the pin is located on the right-front of the green, just below the hump.

To sum up, while it's a short hole, you have to play two precise shots to have a good try at a birdie.

The A Player

This is not a driver hole for you, unless you're proficient at hitting a big fade from the tee. Such a shot, cutting the corner perfectly, might leave you with a sand wedge to the green, but the reward doesn't justify the risk. Catching the trees on the right side is dangerous because not only will you be blocked out, but hitting into them could cause your ball to bounce out of bounds, too. I think your best play is to hit a lofted wood, a 4- or 5-wood, from this tee. You just want to make a smooth controlled pass at it here. Since the tee shot runs slightly downhill, giving you a few extra yards, your normal swing and good contact will put you out there 225 to 230 yards.

Player A makes a nice, relaxed swing with a 4-wood. He expected the shot to be perfect, but the ball draws a little more than he wanted. When he gets to the ball he finds it has landed in the left rough by about a yard. He's 230 yards out from the tee. His line of play has added a little yardage to the hole, but the pin is toward the front, so these points nearly cancel each other and he has 140 yards to the pin.

You're not in bad shape at all here—angle-wise—and the lie is good. Your problem is going to be stopping the ball on the front half of the green, rather than having it run over the hump, leaving you with a very tough putt. So don't take your normal setup and make your normal swing. Here's where having a soft fade in your

In hitting a soft cut-spin fade from rough, align your body well left of the target, your clubface dead at it.

arsenal becomes important. You'll do well to put some fade spin on the ball to give it the soft, "dead" landing you need here, especially since you'll be hitting from light rough.

The distance to the flag is a nice 8-iron for you. Although your lie is good, the ball still may "fly" just a bit. The fade I want you to hit will take about three to five yards off the shot, so these two factors should balance against a slight flyer.

You make or break this shot with your setup. Your feet, knees, hips, and shoulders must all be aligned to the left of your target by about 25 to 30 feet. Your aim will be at about the left-front corner of the green. Meanwhile, you should align the leading edge of your clubface directly at the hole. The key is to take the club back from the ball on a path that's along your body line, which is a shade outside-in in relation to your target line. If you return the clubface square to the target at impact, you'll put a light cut-spin on the shot, so the ball gets up quickly, drifts a shade right in flight, and lands softly. Make a slow, smooth, controlled and deliberate swing in this situation.

The ball starts toward the left side of the green, then drifts a shade right, so that it lands at the front-center and releases to just past pin-high, but below the hump, about 18 feet away from the cup—a well-executed soft fade approach.

Your putt will be quick from just above the hole, and it will break left to right a fairly good amount. In reading the break, remember that a fast putt is going to break much more than a slow putt rolling over the same type of contour since you must hit the fast putt more softly, and the force of gravity will affect a slow-rolling ball much more than a fast-rolling one.

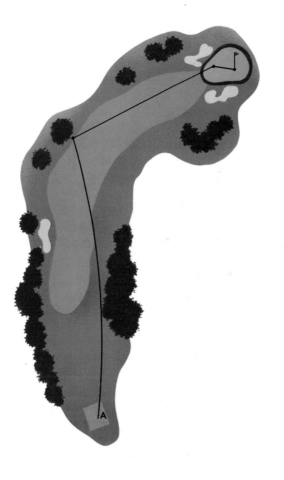

Keeping that in mind, Player A decides to play a full foot of break rather than the eight inches he thought at first glance. He makes sure to start the ball along the intended line, well above the hole, and to keep his head still until the ball's well away. When he looks up, he suspects he's chosen a line that's too "high," but about three feet from the hole the ball swerves just enough to drop softly into the left side.

What a read! You've put your first birdie of the day on your scorecard.

COMMON STRATEGIC AND SHOTMAKING ERRORS BY THE A PLAYER

- Developing a swing path that's too inside-out
- Not playing enough soft shots with the irons

Butch's Lessons

Most A players don't have a problem with slicing the ball. In fact, they often swing the club into the ball a little more from the inside than desirable. This can result in a draw or hook that misses the fairway, even when the swing feels really good. A simple cure if you're drawing too much is to stand about one inch closer to the ball at address. Doing so will help you to push the club straight back from the ball, rather than pulling it inside a little too quickly and returning it too much from the inside, which is the good player's tendency. If that tip doesn't help you, work on the following drill.

DRILL (FOR MAKING A STRAIGHT-BACK INITIAL TAKEAWAY ACTION)

It's critical that, for the first few inches, the club move straight back along the target line. To groove a low one-piece takeaway action, place a tee in the ground about one foot behind the ball you will be addressing.

Next, swing back trying to brush the tee away.

As for your approach, if you hadn't made the setup and swing adjustments I recommended, you almost surely wouldn't have birdied the hole. Your second shot would have carried farther and landed hotter, putting you over the hump and onto the back of the green. You'd have been fortunate to two-putt from there. The ability to play the soft, faded shot to flags cut near the front of the green is a skill that separates the really fine players from the average ones.

The B Player

This hole presents a good par or birdie opportunity for you too. There is no pressure to hit a long tee shot, and if you put it in the fairway, you should have a fairly short iron shot into the green.

If the wind isn't a big factor, a 3-wood is a good choice. You average 210 yards with this club, and since the fairway runs a bit downhill, a 3-wood shot will travel farther than normal, down to where the fairway makes its turn. Make certain to pick a spot of some sort that aligns you down the left-center of the fairway. Aiming a little left is smart because your normal tendency is to fade. Also, with out-of-bounds right, it's always good to shade your shot to the other side of the fairway.

Tee your ball up no more than a half inch and position it in your stance opposite your left heel, maybe an inch back from where you would play it with your driver. Keep the takeaway smooth and your head still.

Player B hits the shot a little thin. The ball starts right of his aiming point, flies low and with a fade, and finishes on the right side of the fairway about 210 yards from the tee. In other words, it's a "good miss." He's far enough out to see the green and he's still on the short grass, with a perfect lie.

With the pin located front-right, you have just over 150 yards to the flag. This is an especially tough shot for you, because you have to be careful not to fade the ball into the bunkers right of the green. You'll be okay, however, if you start your ball well left of the flag, the intention being to let it drift toward the hole and sit down quickly.

All this considered, Player B decides to hit a smooth 5-iron rather than a full 6. Smart thinking. Since a slight fade is his normal shot, this may help him here. I instruct him to align to hit for the center of the green. Again, if the shot fades it will be working toward the hole. I also tell him to choke down the grip just a fraction and try to make a slow, smooth, compact swing.

Player B's ball starts on a line toward the center of the green. However, he contacts the ball just a hair thin, mainly because he stood up through impact, losing the flex in his knees. It's not a bad shot—it's right on line for the center of the green. But it lands about pin-high and is a little "hot," unlike Player A's, so that it scoots over the hump and dribbles just over the back edge, in the apron and about 45 feet from the hole.

You now have a touchy little shot, which you can either putt or chip. The first 20 feet are downhill and fairly fast, then the ball will roll uphill for a few feet to get over the hump, and then take off

down the hump until the last few feet before the hole, which are fairly flat. The shot calls for the ultimate in touch. I'd recommend in this instance you go with the putter, since it's often easier to control the distance on a putt than a chip. Look over the line from several points and concentrate on getting the ball rolling at the proper speed.

Player B tries to do just that, but at the last instant, thinking about getting the ball over the hump, he gives the stroke a little extra juice. Once it gets over the hump he knows he's hit the ball too hard. It slithers past the hole on the right and goes a full 12 feet past. Now, a little rattled, he tries to gather his thoughts and put a good roll on his second putt. The ball pulls up six inches short and he must settle for a bogey.

COMMON STRATEGIC AND SHOTMAKING ERRORS BY THE B PLAYER
- "Coming out of" full shots
- Failing to "read the speed" on comeback putts

Butch's Lessons

When most golfers hit a shot thin or top it, they think the reason is that they lifted their head. This is almost never the actual cause.

Most handicap golfers tend to straighten up on the backswing. This means that if they don't lower their spine angle on the downswing, their arms (and the clubhead) will be a little high coming into the ball. So, eliminate this problem before it starts. Concentrate on swinging around your spine on the backswing rather than lifting the club up. More important, maintain the flex in your knees.

DRILL (FOR STAYING DOWN)

Standing up, or coming out of your flexed knee position through the impact area, leads to mishit shots, mostly weak fades.

To cure this problem, practice hitting shots off downhill lies. Swinging down the slope will encourage you to retain your flex.

How often have you zoomed a downhill putt past the hole, then left the comebacker short? This happens a lot. Remember that after you've just hit a fast downhiller past the cup, your next putt is coming back uphill. You'll probably have to hit the putt a bit more firmly than you think.

To avoid hitting thin iron shots and sending the ball over the green, retain your knee-flex in the hitting area.

The C Player

You, too, can reach this hole in regulation and have high hopes of putting a par-4 score on your card. However, since you're a shorter hitter, you should expect to go with a

---

driver on this hole. If you hit it solidly, you'll get 215 yards with a little downhill roll, which would be sufficient to get around the corner and leave you a clear shot at the green.

Although the hole doglegs right, you want to play down the left side to allow for some fade or slice, and also to put you in play rather than out of bounds if you hit a really big banana ball. Your aim point can be five yards farther left than for the B player. Concentrate on swinging smoothly down your target line.

Impact felt good to Player C, but he left the clubface a little open. The ball sliced with a high flight and landed in the right rough.

You're about 205 yards out from the tee, but you're only 150 from the flag because the hole plays shorter on the line you're on, and the pin is forward. The bad news is, the ball is sitting down slightly in the grass.

This is a situation in which you especially will benefit from having a lofted wood in you bag. This could be numbered either a 7-wood or a 9-wood, and might have a loft of between 24 and 28 degrees. Such a club can really help on shots from the rough at distances anywhere from 165 down to as little as 135 yards.

Let's say you carry a 7-wood. This may be a bit more club than you need from this distance if you catch the ball well, so choke down on the grip one-half inch. Doing this also brings you in a little closer to the ball at address, allowing you to swing on a more upright arc, which is what you want from the rough. Play the ball just ahead of center in your stance and bring the club down steeply into the ball as you would with a short iron. This is still a tough shot, no matter how well you execute, because you're going to meet more resistance at impact than on a shot from the fairway.

Player C hits the shot a little "fat" and realizes immediately it's not going to reach the green. It lands in rough 20 yards short of the bunkers on the right. He's happy, because he's not a good bunker player, but he still has his work cut out. He must play a soft lob over the bunker and stop it quickly since the pin is toward his side of the green.

Since you've got cushion under the ball, take your lob wedge and set the club's leading edge square to the hole. Align your body about 15 degrees to the left. Play the ball a little forward in your stance, opposite your left heel. Take a light grip on the club. You need to play this shot with a relaxed, lazy swing that feels like it's in slow motion. Take a little more swing than you think you need to carry the ball over the bunker.

Player C follows this advice and, surprise—he hits a nice high, soft-landing shot. Because he allowed a margin for error, the ball landed just past pin-high on the left and finished 25 feet past the hole.

That was a good golf shot, especially for a C player. You have a good chance to make 5 on this hole, which is your personal par, despite having been in trouble.

Player C's first putt, though, is a little tentative. It comes up three feet short of the hole.

Don't read added break into this putt, or let your left wrist collapse in the hitting area, as you just did. Make a square-to-square stroke and hit a solid second putt.

You did such a fine job of keeping your head down, and steady, that you didn't see the ball drop into the cup. Good putt and a good 5.

COMMON STRATEGIC AND SHOTMAKING ERRORS BY THE C PLAYER

- Not teeing the ball high enough with the driver
- Letting the left wrist break down on short putts

Butch's Lessons

Many higher handicappers don't know that teeing the ball too low for the driver promotes a slice. The lower you tee the ball, the more upright your swing will tend to be and the greater the tendency to open the clubface through impact. The higher you tee it, the more your swing will tend to move around your body rather than up and down. The slight adjustment in teeing the ball higher will help you bring the clubhead into the ball from inside to along the line, giving you a straighter ball flight.

Many golfers allow the left or lead wrist to break down on short putts, so that the putterblade passes the hands at impact. Concentrate on keeping the left wrist ahead of the putterblade throughout the stroke. This will help you keep the blade low and on line, and allow you to stroke the ball firmly, straight into the cup.

Keeping your left wrist solid will enable you to hit square, solid putts.

DRILL (FOR STOPPING THE LEFT WRIST FROM BREAKING DOWN)

To encourage a firmer left wrist position through impact, try using a unique form of the reverse-overlap putting grip.

Instead of having your left forefinger overlap your right pinky finger, let it drape across the fingers of your right hand.

Practice this grip for about a week, then use it on the course. Not only will your left wrist problem be alleviated, you'll start sinking more short putts.

HOLE	1	2	3	4	5	6	7	8	9	OUT	
YARDS	366	380	485	177	368	373	103	515	356	3123	
PAR	4	4	5	3	4	4	3	5	4	36	
Player A	5	5	5	3	3						
Player B	5	6	5	4	5						
Player C	6	4	8	4	5						

HOLE	10	11	12	13	14	15	16	17	18	IN	TOTAL
YARDS	183	508	121	339	339	417	407	452	510	3276	6399
PAR	3	5	3	4	4	4	4	4	5	36	72
Player A											
Player B											
Player C											

SEMINOLE GOLF CLUB
Par 4: 373 yards

The 6th hole on this tour, from the superb course at Seminole on Florida's Atlantic coast, is one of several examples in this book of superior par-4 holes that are by no means overpowering in length. Seminole's 6th measures only 383 yards even from the championship tees, short enough that a monster driver like Tiger Woods could entertain the thought of ripping his driver directly at the green—though that wouldn't be any smarter for Tiger than it would be for the rest of us. For us mere mortals who must take two full swings to cover this distance, number 6 is a masterpiece of strategic design. The great Ben Hogan, not one to toss compliments around lightly, has been quoted as saying that it is "the best par four hole in the world."

Seminole, built in the 1920s by Donald Ross, was the first great golf course to be constructed in the Deep South. It features large, exceptionally true Bermuda greens that average between 7500 and 8000 square feet, and its flat landscape is dominated by some 200 bunkers. When the wind blows off the Atlantic as it usually does, the course offers a stiff challenge. I must also add with a great deal of pride that the course record, a 12-under-par 60, is claimed by my father, Claude Harmon, and that fantastic score has held up for almost 50 years, since 1948.

But let's get back to number 6. This medium-length hole can't quite be called a dogleg. However, the fairway angles to the left in relation to the teeing area. To the left of the landing area runs a series of huge fairway bunkers; the first one, which is by far the largest, cuts into the fairway and begs you to cut its corner. The more you can cut off, the shorter the hole will play, and you'll also have a much better angle into the deep but extremely narrow green.

As you look out from the tee with that imposing vista of sand on the left, though, your first thought is to keep your tee ball safely right. And you also have to keep in mind that the prevailing wind off the Atlantic blows from left to right on this hole. This makes for a strong tendency to bail out on the tee shot, so you wind up missing the fairway right, ending up either in the palmettos down that side of the hole or catching the single right-side fairway bunker. In short, the 6th at Seminole calls for a very exacting tee shot with a right-to-left draw to counteract the wind and accommodate the left-bending angle of the fairway.

The iron shot into the green, by contrast, asks the golfer to fade the ball. Four more intimidating bunkers angle in from the right side of the green to a point in the fairway about 50 yards in front of it, with two more bunkers on the left. The green, narrow as it is, opens up at a left-to-right angle in relation to the line of the fairway, so approach shots fading in from left to right have a better chance of hitting and holding the putting surface. The net result is that to play this hole perfectly you need to hit two shotmaker's shots in a row that are exactly the opposite of each other. This may be a little bit beyond your capabilities, so let's take a look now at how each level of player should plan to play this outstanding hole.

The A Player

Given the modest length of the hole as well as the precision it requires, the first rule of thumb for the A player, unless you happen to be tremendously confident in your driving accuracy, is to leave the big stick in the bag. It's always harder to hit the fairway with a driver than with a more lofted club, of course. But it's even more difficult to hit a controlled draw with a driver, as this hole requires, when the prevailing wind is blowing from left to right. I strongly recommend you hit a 3-wood here, or even a more lofted wood or a 2-iron if you're more confident with one of these clubs. Your normal 235 yards with a well-struck 3-wood will leave you a short iron to the green, and even if you go with a little shorter club from the tee, you should still be left with a very manageable distance to the flag.

Player A went with the 3-wood, but swung too fast. The ball finished on the right side of the fairway.

There's no real problem here. You have 140 to 145 yards left to the middle of the green (the hole plays a few yards longer from this angle), and that translates to an 8-iron. However, from this angle your view is impeded by the bunkers cutting in from the right, so

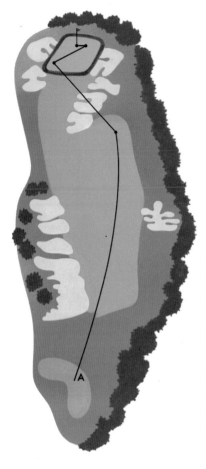

that the precise distance to the flag is harder to judge. Without delaying play, walk over toward the left side of the fairway to get a better look at both the line to the flag and its depth. You're a good enough player that you should know your yardages exactly. You see that the flag is five yards back from the green's center, so compute this into your total yardage figure.

Before you set up to the shot, double-check the wind's direction and velocity. The prevailing left-to-right wind means you'll need to align yourself and your clubface a little left of where you want the ball to finish. Also, keep in mind that a crosswind may take a few yards off the shot's carry, so you might need one more club. Finally, this is the type of shot where the controlled, three-quarter iron swing will come in handy, since you have a better chance of keeping a lower-flight short iron on line than a high one.

Player A makes a good swing, but because he underclubbed, his shot never reaches the hole. Still, he hits the green, although he faces a long birdie putt.

Player A leaves his approach putt on the low side of the hole. His direction is bad, but the fact that the ball finishes hole-high proves his pace is perfect. He holes out his next putt for par.

COMMON STRATEGIC AND SHOTMAKING ERRORS BY THE A PLAYER

- Swinging too fast on the drive
- Underclubbing on the approach shot
- Poor direction control on approach putts

Butch's Lessons

A good breeze blowing from left to right, at the back of the right-handed player, is a tough one to handle. There's a tendency in such conditions to rush the start of the downswing, jerking the club down with the hands. This rushed downswing generally leads to missed and, particularly, pulled shots. So if you're playing this hole in a left-to-right wind, remind yourself to keep the entire swing on a nice level pace.

DRILL (FOR FINDING YOUR IDEAL SWING TEMPO)

You're one of those players who have trouble swinging the driver at an even pace. Most of the time you get quick, particularly when playing into a headwind or a left-to-right crosswind. This practice drill should help you find "your" tempo.

Divide thirty balls evenly into six separate piles.

Hit all five in the first pile, noting the distance and direction of each ball's flight, and how well you stay balanced.

Move on to pile number two, trying to hit the balls five yards farther, keeping in mind that it's a faster lower-body rotation (knees and hips) that generates additional distance, not a harder arm swing. If the balls travel longer and stay pretty straight, and you retained your balance, move on to pile three, and try to add another five yards.

If you are still in balance and you hit longer on-target tee shots, move on to pile four.

Once you get to the point where you feel out of balance, are unable to control the club, and mishit shots, you have hit your personal wall. Back off one notch from there, and that's as hard as you can and should swing the "big stick."

An approach shot from the right side of the fairway is tricky because the bunkers in the fairway fronting the green can keep you from judging just how far it is to the front of the green (and, of course, to the pin). The shot may very well look shorter than it is as you stand over your approach, so that you're tempted to choose what will end up being too little club. Make up your mind ahead of time to get your precise yardage, then trust that yardage and pick the correct club to fly the ball to the hole.

In this case, Player A should have played a controlled shot with a 7-iron, instead of hitting a normal full shot with an 8-iron. That way, the ball would have ridden the wind to the right, toward the hole.

On his approach putt, had Player A picked an interim target along his line (e.g., a light spot of grass, or maybe a point just inside one), then set his putterface square to it, he would have likely tracked the ball along a path to the high side of the hole. On a breaking putt, you want to decide on the high point of the arc of the putt, then choose a spot directly between your ball and that point to aim at. This gets the putt started on line, and increases its chance of falling into the "side door," on the high side.

The B Player

Even though you're going to hit the tee shot shorter than the A player, I still recommend that under normal conditions you go with a 3-wood from this tee. The reasoning is similar: It's easier to draw the ball with your 3-wood than with a driver, and since the left-to-right wind will make a fade fly much farther right, a draw makes it much easier to find this fairway in particular. Also, the more to the left you can keep your tee shot while staying out of the bunker, the better your opening to the flag on your approach.

Alignment on the tee shot is important, and never more so than on this type of winding, awkward hole. And good alignment is trickier to come by whenever the fairway is bending in the landing area. You need to aim to a spot in the part of the fairway where you expect your ball to land. In this example, if you make solid contact with the 3-wood, you can expect a carry and roll of about 215 yards. Knowing this, you should aim your tee shot just a shade farther right than the long driver who expects to hit it, say, 260. The long hitter's correct line would call for a shot that starts farther left, carrying more of that first gigantic fairway bunker.

Player B does everything right and sends his tee shot soaring down the center line. However, the ball drifts a little right with the breeze instead of drawing, and finishes on the right edge of the fairway. Player B is 215 yards from the tee, but because the hole is playing a little longer along this line than the yardage on the card, he has about 165 yards left to the middle of the green. Although on the same line as Player A was, Player B faces a longer shot. He has at least a 5-iron left and possibly a 4. Plus, he'll have to play this approach directly over at least two of the bunkers that jut in front of the green from the right.

After taking a look at the shot from the left side of the fairway to get a better look at the exact target, as I recommended for the A player, Player B decides to go with the 4-iron. With the opening to the green on the left, the ideal shot would be a normal 4-iron aimed at the left bunker.

Player B swings. The ball "balloons" in the wind, drifting wildly to the right, until it finally comes to rest in the greenside bunker to the right of the green.

You might call it rotten luck, but I would say you've been trapped by the design of a great hole. You didn't aim far enough left of the pin, plus you hit the ball too high.

Making Player B's position even more precarious is the fact that the bunker to

Good players don't chip the ball out of sand. Instead, they hit a blast shot, letting the sand lift the ball out.

the right of the green here is very deep. The shot here is out of this deep bunker, up a steep slope, and to a pin on the short side of a very skinny green. He tries to cut under and through the sand, but blades the ball instead, sending it running across the green and into the far fringe, where he takes two shots to get down. Score:

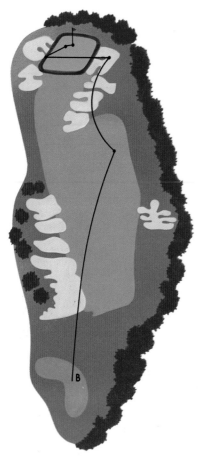

bogey 5. He could have done better had he blasted the ball and let the sand lift the ball gently into the air. Still, for him he scored a "personal par."

COMMON STRATEGIC AND SHOT-MAKING ERRORS BY THE B PLAYER

- Not aiming left of the pin and hitting the ball too high
- Failing to open the blade enough on the greenside sand shot

Butch's Lessons

It's so easy to get into the habit of aiming your iron shots straight at the pin. On great courses, you have to be much more careful and aware. Since the green opening is well left of the pin from the angle you are shooting, plus the fact that the wind will probably help the ball right, you should have tried to start your shot at the left corner of the green or about 30 feet left of the flag. Also, it would have helped if you had hit a lower shot; you had the ball off your left instep, and that position promoted the high shot you hit. Next time, move the ball back in your stance, so it's a couple of inches behind your left heel. This position will promote a stronger shot that won't be affected quite so much by the left-to-right wind.

Any time you choose to chip from a bunker, you run the risk of hitting the ball over the green (or flubbing the shot). Watch the pros closely on basic greenside sand shots. They'll play them with the clubface laid wide open. This allows them to skim the club through the sand, so the ball is lifted up softly by the blast. Using the flange of the sand wedge correctly is particularly important in Florida sand, which is generally softer and deeper.

The C Player

Since it's just 373 yards, the 6th at Seminole gives the C player high hopes for a par. A good drive of 210 yards will put the green well within reach in two. The trick, of course, is to execute the two exacting shots it will take to get on the green in regulation.

Unlike my advice to the A and B players, I suggest you go ahead and give the driver a try on this hole, for two reasons: First, you'll need your full distance from the tee. If you hit less than a driver here, you'll have a tough, long shot to the green, if you can get there at all. Also, as a shorter hitter you will have some concern about carrying the corner of that first, monstrous fairway bunker with less than a driver.

Player C gives the driver a rip, but at the last second the image of that intimidating line of bunkers on the left flashes into his mind. Instead of releasing freely through impact, he "holds on" to the club, leaving the face open at impact even more than usual. He hits a block slice about 190 yards, into the rough and about 20 yards right of the fairway.

Next time let your right forearm and hand release freely over your left through impact. That way you'll hit a draw instead of a block. Keeping your right heel down through impact will also help your arms release properly.

A possible disaster hole is looming. But Player C catches a break when he finds that the ball is sitting down just slightly. Here, though, is where a lot of high-handicappers shoot themselves in the foot. They think, "I'm 180 or 190 yards out. I can get there with a 3-wood."

Well, wait a minute. You'd have to hit your career shot out of an imperfect lie with your longest fairway club, to carry over a line of bunkers and land the ball on a well-guarded green. Even a Tour player would have trouble with this shot. Put that club away and start playing smart golf instead.

You should estimate the distance between your ball and the bunker in the center of the fairway that starts about 50 yards from the green—about 130 yards. You should play a low, controlled punch shot from out of the rough with perhaps a 5- or 6-iron, hit-

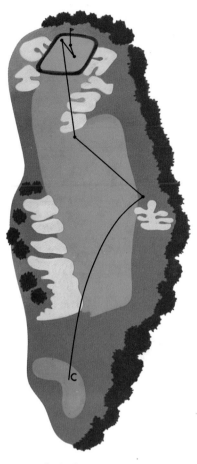

ting it 110 or 120 yards. This will put you in the fairway but short of the first bunker. Ideally, you would want to try to hit the left side of the fairway to set up the easiest pitch shot.

Player C hits the ball down the middle of the fairway, 10 yards short of the bunker. That's fine. He now faces a long pitch over the line of bunkers, with about 75 yards to the hole.

You'll want to hit a high, soft-landing shot to get the ball close. Here again, though, is where many high-handicappers misexecute. In an effort to get extra loft on the ball, they try to open the face of their pitching or sand wedge through impact, rather than simply making a solid swing. The result is that they not only make contact with an overlofted clubface, but also decelerate through impact. Instead of carrying the needed distance, they drop the ball well short; on this hole, that means into one of the bunkers.

Instead of "babying" your wedges, try this: Line up slightly open toward your target (again, it's wise to aim about 10 feet left of the hole here), with your ball virtually centered in a narrow stance. Forget about trying to hit a soft shot. Instead, take the nice three-quarter swing that this distance requires. Release the clubhead freely through the ball as with a normal iron shot. As your clubface moves beyond impact, close it naturally rather than hang on to the club so you leave the face open and bloop the ball weakly.

Player C hits his pitch crisply, over the bunkers and safely on, a little bit long and left of the pin but still with a 20-foot putt for his par. Not bad. But he gets too carried away with his relative success and goes gunning for his par putt. He knocks the ball several feet by, but concentrates hard on his comebacker, and holes it for a well-earned bogey 5.

COMMON SHOTMAKING AND STRATEGIC ERRORS BY THE C PLAYER

- Steering the swing
- Trying too hard to make long par putts and three-putting instead

Butch's Lessons

When standing on the tee readying yourself to drive, don't stare at the hazards lining the fairway. This preswing misdeed causes you to steer the swing so that you miss one hazard on one side of the fairway and hit the ball into trouble on the other side of the fairway. Instead, focus your eyes intently on your target area. This positive preswing routine, coupled with a mental image of the proper release action, will raise your level of confidence and promote a powerfully accurate shot.

Forming a vivid mental image of a fluid hands-arms-club release action, before you swing, will promote powerfully accurate shots.

Don't get carried away with the thought of holing putts of 20 feet or more in your eagerness to make as many pars as possible. If you putt too boldly, you'll end up 3-putting more than 1-putting. Concentrate on speed first and line second. If your middle-range putts consistently carry the right speed, a much higher percentage of them will drop.

HOLE	1	2	3	4	5	6	7	8	9	OUT	
YARDS	366	380	485	177	368	373	103	515	356	3123	
PAR	4	4	5	3	4	4	3	5	4	36	
Player A	5	5	5	3	3	4					
Player B	5	6	5	4	5	5					
Player C	6	4	8	4	5	5					
HOLE	10	11	12	13	14	15	16	17	18	IN	TOTAL
YARDS	183	508	121	339	339	417	407	452	510	3276	6399
PAR	3	5	3	4	4	4	4	4	5	36	72
Player A											
Player B											
Player C											

When I think of bold red wines, robust Cuban cigars, the roar of a Ferrari engine, or the powerful voice of an opera singer, I think of Pebble Beach, a course that is bigger than life. Its great expanses of green grass, steep rocky cliffs, tall cypress trees, and the unforgettable bright blue Pacific Ocean lying on the lip of this magnificent wonderful layout, make it unquestionably the most beautiful course in all of golf. Pebble Beach, to me, is the eighth wonder of the world.

"Pebble," as golf aficionados refer to this spectacular course, is located in California's Monterey Peninsula. It's about 120 miles south of San Francisco, along the craggy shore of Carmel Bay. Not surprisingly, Robert Louis Stevenson, the author of *Treasure Island*, once referred to this spot on the globe as "the most felicitous meeting of land and sea in Creation."

When course designer Jack Neville and his collaborator Douglas Grant unveiled Pebble Beach in 1919, they must have stood back and said, "We've done it," with the same exhausted joy that filled the heart of Michelangelo on completing the ceiling of the Sistine Chapel. What they didn't know is that Pebble would be photographed more times than Marilyn Monroe, be ranked the greatest course in the world several times, host United States Amateur and Open Championships, and bring so much joy to so many golfers around the world, including the pros and amateurs who compete each January in the AT&T Pebble Beach National Pro-Am.

The AT&T was originally the Bing Crosby National Pro-Am, a tournament that itself evolved from an annual clambake that Crosby put together for his golfing buddies and friends from the entertainment world. This event, maybe more than any other, helped popularize golf in America, especially when they started televising it.

Before Crosby got involved with Pebble it was basically a playground resort for the rich. Today, anyone can play Pebble, considered to be the best public course in America.

From the time you tee off on hole number 1, to the time you play the famous par-5 18th running along the Pacific, you will be awestruck by the scenery and the challenge that Pebble Beach Golf Links offers.

Pebble's uniqueness is highlighted by one hole in particular, the par-3 7th, a hole that is truly one of a kind. In fact, many golf experts say it is the best par 3 in the world. Just listen to the way the late American golf writer Charles Price described this little tester in *The World Atlas of Golf*:

There is no finer short hole than the 7th at Pebble Beach. After mounting the crest of the 6th, the golfer turns towards the ocean. There below him on a promontory, bounded with rocks where the surf spills silver, lies a tiny green of 2000 square feet embraced by sand. The hole measures only 120 yards (from the back tees) and is downhill. In calm air a wedge or 9-iron is the club, but when the wind is strong from the Pacific, golfers may be fingering medium irons to keep the ball low on line. Normally the shot offers no problem to the expert, but the distance is not easy to judge and there are no marks for being too bold. The heaving tumult of the waves awaits. Short the hole may be, but even great players must thrill to the sight of the ball fighting high against the sky and falling softly near the flag. This requires the utmost precision because the green lies directly along the line of the approach and offers a target of no more than eight yards in width.

Mr. Price is absolutely correct in suggesting that club selection at Pebble's 7th hole is of paramount importance. It's unlike many other par-3 holes that allow you to hit a slightly off-line shot and still hit the green. Make the smallest error here and you miss the green. Therefore, before you take a club out of your bag, carefully consider the direction and strength of the wind, and remind yourself that when hitting downhill you need less club than when hitting to a green that's level with the tee. In other words, if you usually hit a 9-iron, play a pitching wedge. On this hole, it's also better to be short than long. So, if caught between two clubs, play the shorter one. Okay, enough advice; let's see if 7 is your lucky number.

The A Player

I gave you perfect marks for the way you set up (ball back, hands ahead) and executed the shot, particularly with that 10-mph wind at your back. Your preswing routine was textbook, and an example for all B and C players to follow. You carefully considered the course conditions, picked the right club, made a smooth practice swing, and aimed your body and club correctly. I was particularly happy to see you account for the helping wind, choose the sand wedge over the pitching wedge, and employ an even-tempoed rhythmic swing. Yes, you're right, the work did pay off. Not many pros hit a soft punch under the wind, to 15 feet. On the negative side, I did have a problem with the way you handled the birdie putt and had to settle for par.

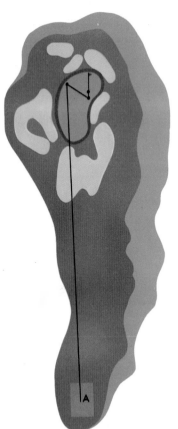

COMMON STRATEGIC AND SHOT-MAKING ERRORS BY THE A PLAYER

- Not reading the putt correctly
- Not making a solid stroke

Butch's Lessons

I could see that you were confused about the break in the green, simply because you took so long to stand up to the ball and putt. Further, when you did hit it, you sort of made a lazy wristy stroke rather than a confident arms-shoulders controlled action. That's why your birdie putt drifted off on the low side.

Pay close attention to the way a putt breaks, including the green's grain; this is the way that all scratch players and pro golfers think before putting. Start "reading" the green when you're about 15 yards from it. You'll be surprised what you notice, particularly in the late afternoon. As you mark the ball, peek at the line to the hole to get a preliminary idea of how the ball will roll. Next, check the line from behind the hole, and once again from behind the ball, only this time more carefully, so that you get a clearer picture of any subtle breaks in the green. Next, look at the line from both sides, also paying close attention to the grain. If there is a sheen to the grass, the putt is down-grain and will run faster than normal. If the grass is dull, you are putting against the grain, so expect the ball to roll more slowly.

If you are truly in doubt about how the putt breaks, plumb-bob the line. Here's how to do it:

Stand behind the ball, facing the hole. Next, hold the putter at arm's length in front of you with only your right thumb and forefinger, so that it hangs vertically. Obscure the view of the ball with the lower part of the shaft, then close your nondominant eye. If the hole now appears to be to the left of the shaft, the putt will break to the left. If the hole appears to be to the right of the shaft, it will break from left to right. If the shaft appears to also cover the hole, the putt is dead straight.

This whole process may seem laborious, but it will not take you long once you get used to it. Besides, once you see that it pays off on undulating greens, you'll make the plumb-bob process part of your preparatory routine.

Knowing that you have figured the break correctly will heighten your confidence, thereby encouraging you to make a smooth, one-piece, wristless stroke. One more thing: When you're sure of the break and how hard to stroke the ball, be sure to focus on the starting line of the putt and to align the face of the putter squarely to it.

The B Player

Player B spent some time over in Scotland, and he played college golf in Texas, so he knew exactly how to handle the wind. Taking a pitching wedge out of the bag, he teed the ball about an inch off the ground, played the ball back slightly in his stance, made a three-quarter swing, and hit a shot just inside the spot where Player A's

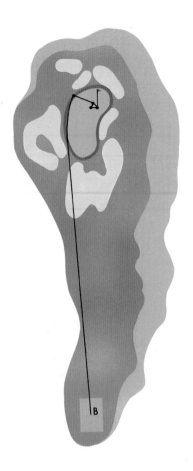

ball came to rest. He must have been listening to what I said, or he just knew what he was doing. In any case, he read the break perfectly, but the ball missed by a whisker, spinning off the left side of the cup and running about two feet by, in what's called tap-in range. Oh, he missed the tap-in! Bogey 4.

COMMON STRATEGIC AND SHOT-MAKING ERRORS BY THE B PLAYER

- Not giving a short putt 100 percent concentration
- Not taking enough time to prepare to putt

Butch's Lessons

Believe it or not, some of the most strategically smart, careful players in the game (including three-time U.S. Open champion Hale Irwin) have missed short tap-in putts because they took the shot for granted and rushed their routine.

It's one thing that you got mad after you missed the putt for birdie, but it's worse that you rushed your par putt. You walked right over to the ball and didn't even settle into your standard setup. You simply brushed the putterblade at the ball, as if you were playing hockey.

Proceed with caution on short putts. Treat them like any other putt. Mark your ball, clean it, reset it down, look at the line, get set, then putt. As I told Tiger, don't worry about missing. We've all been careless and missed tap-ins. Just learn your lesson.

The C Player

When I saw you select the pitching
wedge, address the ball so professionally,
and make a smooth compact backswing, I
thought you were surely going to hit a
good shot. But a sequence of incorrect
downswing movements caused you to hit
the ball into the left trap.

You got a bad break hitting into a
"fried-egg" lie in the sand. However,
choosing the wrong club and employing
the wrong technique caused you to
waste a shot by hitting over the green.

In the trap, you set the pitching
wedge's clubface square to the target,
and employed a short hit-and-hold action. This is how you should play the
shot when the ball is sitting down in a
regular buried lie, and when you have
around 30 feet of green to work with.
But the lie you faced presents different
demands. The ball was not only

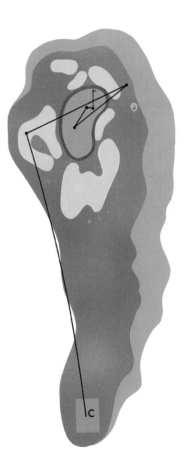

plugged, but also surrounded by a circular wall of sand. Further, you had very little green between the ball and the hole. In such circumstances, you can't afford to hit the ball with added overspin. I'll show you how to handle this lie shortly.

Perhaps in frustration, you didn't make your best effort on the chip you faced, using an exaggerated hand action and running the ball well past the hole. The fried-egg lie was a bad break, but it was this poor chip running over the green that led to two putts and a double-bogey.

COMMON STRATEGIC AND SHOTMAKING ERRORS BY THE C PLAYER

- Incorrect downswing action
- Not knowing how to handle a unique lie in sand

Butch's Lessons

You pulled the ball into the trap located on the left side of the green because of a combination of downswing faults. You left your weight on your right side. You let your right shoulder jut outward, ahead of your left. You pulled the club down violently, and across the target line, with your hands.

On shots like this, simply nudge your body weight onto your left foot and leg at the start of the downswing. Think: "gentle shift." The arms and hands will follow the lead of the lower body and bring the club squarely into the ball. Slow down your tempo, too, because with the wind behind, an easy Mark O'Meara-style swing is all you need.

Whenever the ball is in a fried-egg lie, like the one shown here, and you have limited green to work with, select a sand wedge. Lay the clubface wide open, setting it behind the "white" of the imaginary egg. Make an extra-wristy three-quarter backswing. Blast out the white by digging the club deeply into the sand, about three inches behind the ball, then follow through fully.

The first step in recovering from a fried-egg lie is opening the clubface and setting it directly behind the "yolk."

In addressing your chipping problems, think of your hands, arms, wrists, and shoulders as one connected triangle. While keeping your body practically perfectly still, swing the club back in one piece, let-ting the imaginary triangle control the action. Only on longer chips do I suggest adding a tiny bit of wrist action to your stroke, since it promotes added feel for distance. Otherwise, quiet both the hands and wrists. Let the loft of the club lift the ball into the air; don't ever try to help the ball up. When you do that, the tendency is to quicken the downswing and hit the ball well past the hole.

HOLE	1	2	3	4	5	6	7	8	9	OUT	
YARDS	366	380	485	177	368	373	103	515	356	3123	
PAR	4	4	5	3	4	4	3	5	4	36	
Player A	5	5	5	3	3	4	3				
Player B	5	6	5	4	5	5	4				
Player C	6	4	8	4	5	5	5				

HOLE	10	11	12	13	14	15	16	17	18	IN	TOTAL
YARDS	183	508	121	339	339	417	407	452	510	3276	6399
PAR	3	5	3	4	4	4	4	4	5	36	72
Player A											
Player B											
Player C											

Inverness Club, located in Toledo, Ohio, is a classic old club that has played a large part in the early lore of golf in America. Inverness originated as a nine-hole course in 1903. Sixteen years later, a second nine was built by Donald Ross, and it has several times since undergone other remodeling efforts.

Inverness has tremendous character. The most notable feature of its design is the course's smallish, well-bunkered greens, which require approach shots that are struck with pinpoint accuracy. Another interesting aspect of the course is that it has just three par 3s and only two par 5s (one of which we'll be playing here); the other thirteen holes are all par 4s, including the final five. That gives Inverness a par of 71, and since the course has grown over the years to where it's now listed at 7024 yards from the tournament tees, it is an excellent championship test. The U.S. Open was held at Inverness four times between 1920 and 1979; in 1993 it hosted the PGA Championship, won by Paul Azinger in a dramatic playoff over Greg Norman after the two had tied at 12-under-par 272.

The second par 5 of your round is the 8th hole at Inverness. It is the number five handicap hole on the course. You'll be playing it at 515 yards, a fairly manageable length (it's 554 yards from the tournament tees). As you may be able to tell from the opening photograph and the schematic showing the design of this hole, the key shot is the drive. You have no choice but to hit it pretty straight here—for the first 140 yards the fairway is hemmed in by tall trees on both sides. Once you get out of the chutelike driving area, the hole doglegs to the left, and also begins to open up some. The second shot moves slightly uphill to an area where fairway bunkers stand ready to catch errant shots. So, for the majority of golfers who are laying up, the second shot must be played with care.

Let's keep in mind, though, that when played from a length of 515 yards, the hole may be reachable in two for some power hitters. This is particularly true since the fairway moves downhill to the green for the last 100 yards or so.

The medium-sized green is well guarded by large, deep bunkers on both sides, so the short iron or wedge third shot that many players will face can't be taken for granted. This green (as are all at Inverness) is full of subtle contours and you must read it carefully. Still, this is a hole where birdies are a good possibility for the A player, and even the C player has an excellent chance to hit the green in three and have a go at a birdie as well.

The A Player

This is a good example of a hole where it pays to start your planning from the green and then work your way back toward the tee, a course management strategy I've worked on with Tiger Woods. The wind isn't much of a factor today. That being the case, you may have a shot at getting home in two. The green is well guarded, but you're a pretty good bunker player so the greenside traps are not a real threat. If you were to go for the green in two and land in one of the bunkers, you'd probably still have a better chance of making a birdie than you would by laying up and playing a full third shot in. All this, of course, leads you back to the tee, where the correct choice for you is to hit the driver.

This tee shot, although a difficult one, sets up well for you because this hole calls for a draw in order to keep the ball in the fairway and shave off a little distance. Tee the ball a little higher than normal, as this promotes a right-to-left draw. Move the club back from the ball slowly—this is always good advice, but especially when you're trying to hit a powerful tee shot.

Player A's action looked good, but his backswing plane was too flat and he used a little too much wrist action on the downswing. These minor faults caused him to turn the ball over in an exaggerated right-to-left shot pattern. Fortunately, the ball flew by the last big tree bordering the left side of the fairway and came to rest in the rough.

You should swing on a rounded plane when trying to hit a draw. Just be careful not to let the club get so far behind you. Taking the club straight back along the target line will help you correct your plane problem. Work on that drill I recommended to you on hole 5. Concentrating harder on making a fluid arm swing on the way down will help tame your wrists.

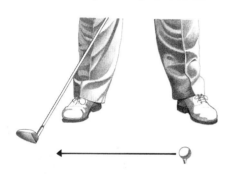

To avoid swinging on an overly flat plane, take the club straight back along the target line (or only slightly inside it) during the initial stage of backswing.

Because you hit the shot solidly and gained extra carry and roll from the right-to-left flight, the ball has traveled 260 yards. Also, since you've cut some 15 yards off the hole by going down the left edge, you have only 240 yards left to the green, and your lie is reasonably good. Should you go for the green? If you were going to lay up, you would want to be about 110 yards from the green, so you could hit a nice pitching wedge from a level lie. But that would mean you'd only need to punch an 8- or 9-iron for your second shot. If you are able to make good contact with a 4- or 5-wood, and the ball "jumps" a bit from the light rough, you can still get home in two. Since there are no major penalties such as water or out of bounds to contend with, this is a good opportunity to go for it.

Because Player A was aware of the lie in the rough and didn't want the clubface of his 4-wood to turn over, he succumbed to the tendency to leave the face open on this shot and hit a "block" to the right. The ball flew high and slightly shorter than if he'd caught it with the face square, so that the shot landed short of the right-front bunker, in the rough. He now faces a short pitch of about 35 yards to the hole, which is cut in the right-center of the green.

Your gamble didn't pay off, and you have a touchy shot, but you still should be able to at least put your third on the green with a decent putt at a birdie. Your lie in the rough is fair. You'll need to play an extra-soft, extra-high super-cut shot to carry the bunkers and stop the ball near the hole. Here's how to do it: First, select your lob wedge if you carry one (your sand wedge if you don't). Position the ball forward in the stance, opposite your left instep. Align your body about 10 feet to the left of the hole, while aiming the leading edge of your wedge a shade to the right of the flag. Make a slow, smooth, long backswing for the length of shot at hand, making sure to keep your head steady. Swing the club down along your body line, making sure to accelerate the arms through impact. You should feel as though you're slicing the clubface underneath the ball with your right hand. The outside-in path of your

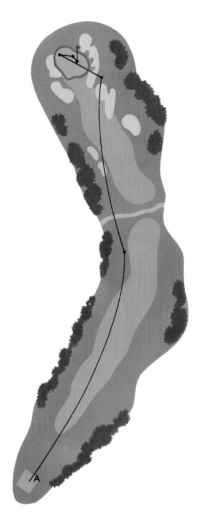

swing plus the open clubface should give the ball a high, soft flight.

Player A's shot lands short of pin high and left of it, then releases slightly to finish 20 feet past the hole. From there, he two-putts for par. Not a bad score, but frankly he should have given himself a much better opportunity to score birdie.

COMMON STRATEGIC AND SHOTMAKING ERRORS BY THE A PLAYER

- Not using the teeing area to your advantage
- Not imparting enough cut-spin on the ball when playing a lob

Butch's Lessons

Your hooked tee shot barely got by the last tree on the left. Since you know that you want to play a right-to-left shot from the tee, and particularly because this is a tight driving hole, you should tee the ball up on the left side of the teeing area. This will automatically help you align your tee shot to start down the right-center of the fairway, which is what you want when trying to draw the shot for extra distance.

It's become fashionable around the green to try the super-cut shot made famous by Phil Mickelson and also by Tiger Woods. This is where you take a full swing at the ball with the clubface wide open, so that the ball goes almost straight up and stops dead. Basically, you did a fine job of hitting this shot, with one exception: you failed to swing the club along your body line. As a result, you didn't impart sufficient cut-spin on the ball; that's why it ran by the hole, rather than stopping quickly.

The B Player

You, too, should plan your play on this par 5 by working back from green to tee, to determine the best combination of shots to give you a birdie putt. However, your tee shot strategy will be slightly different from Player A's. You can't realistically get home in two. You should try, instead, to set up the best possible third shot. On this hole, that would be a wedge or 9-iron from the left-center of the fairway, short of the left bunkers that are about 100 yards from the middle of the green. You'll gain no advantage from trying to get your second shot closer to the green, because the shorter pitch from a downhill lie would be trickier. Also, if you don't hit your long second as well as you plan, you could hit the ball into one of the three fairway bunkers—which you definitely want to avoid. So, really, all you want to do on this hole is hit your first two shots straight, a total of between 380 and 400 yards. There's no sense in trying to press for more. That being the case, your club of choice off the tee should be a 3-wood. This makes particular sense because the tee shot is narrow. Also, since you tend to fade your drives, this hole doesn't set up as well for you as for the A player, so you want a little more margin for error. Set up for the shot from the right-center of the tee box. You just want to make a slow, smooth swing and make solid contact that will give you 210 to 220 yards with this club.

Player B failed to release the club properly. As I thought, it was because he tightened his grip on the club as he started the down-swing. As a result, the clubface was open at impact, and that caused the ball to fly right of target. "Grabbing" on the downswing is a fairly common error among amateurs, especially on tight driving holes. Most people don't even know they're doing it. At any rate, Player B's shot faded. The good news: Because his shot started out at the proper angle, it flew past the tree line okay, but it slid several yards into the right rough. He's not in bad shape at all at 215 yards out, with a clear shot and a fair lie in light rough.

Your main concern on your second shot is to keep clear of the fairway bunkers on the left and right sides. You're playing your second somewhat diagonally, from the right rough back to the left; a good tip here is to use the left-hand bunkers as your target. This is a case where you want to stay away from the right side, and also stay short of the left-hand bunkers. Select a club that you know you can't get to the left bunkers with, then hit at the first of the two. Your normal 5-iron distance, for example, is 160 yards; however, it will probably fly a bit from this lie. Keep your head still and drive the club aggressively down and through the ball.

Player B hits the shot solid and straight—the ball gets some extra run and goes 170 yards, finishing on the left side of the fairway.

You're in great shape, 130 yards from the flag, with a good angle to it. This is normally an 8-iron for you; however, the shot is a little downhill so it will play about five yards shorter. Choke down on your 8-iron grip a half inch, align yourself at the center of the green just left of the pin, then swing normally.

Player B hits the ball left of target, because he swung too fast. However, since he had plenty of club, the ball clears the bunkers with room to spare and finishes pin-high, 30 feet away. Even though Player B hit two shots (of the three he played) that weren't

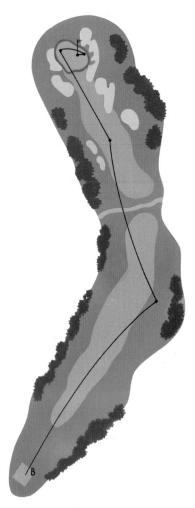

his best, he's still putting for birdie thanks to good course management.

His putt is more or less sidehill, and he reads a two-foot break to the right on the fast green. He hits the putt solidly, but it stays about six inches on the high side and goes two feet past. Not bad, but he now faces a down-hiller that's not a "gimme." Here, it's almost always best to play the ball inside the hole and putt it firmly into the back, taking any slight breaks out of the equation. He makes no mistakes and raps the ball into the back of the cup for a well-earned par 5.

COMMON STRATEGIC AND SHOT-MAKING ERRORS BY THE B PLAYER

- Not using hazards as signposts
- Failing to hit control shots with the short irons

Butch's Lessons

On your second shot, you utilized the first left-side fairway bunker as a target, because I was there to guide you. Many golfers don't realize that course architects often use distant bunkers as much for directional guides for tee shots or long second shots, as they do for trapping people. Take a good look at the bunkering on your home course and you may see that some of them really act as good targets.

Most middle-level amateurs would play much better if they learned to hit their short and middle-distance approach shots with a controlled action rather than at nearly 100 percent of full power. This is one of the most important things I've taught Tiger Woods, and it's responsible for a lot of the great improvement in his game since his early college days. It's hard to believe that Tiger's not hitting the ball at full power, but he's not—and there's really no loss of distance from hitting the ball at 75 percent of full effort. You'll find that your balance is so much better and your contact more precise, and most important, the shots that you don't quite hit flush will find the green a lot more often than your misses will when you swing all-out.

The C Player

Your strategy from the tee will be pretty much the same as the B player's—that is, you want to hit two solid shots that leave you with a clear shot-iron third shot and a chance for, at worst, a two-putt par.

Since the tee shot is tight, even though you are a shorter hitter than the B player, you may want to go with a 3-wood off the tee. You normally get just about 200 yards with this club, so you could get enough distance with a fairway wood second to get within comfortable range of the green with your third. Go with the 3-wood.

This is a hole where you'd dearly love to hit a nice right-to-left draw off the tee, both to fit the shape of the hole and also to add some distance. Most high-handicap players, who usually do not

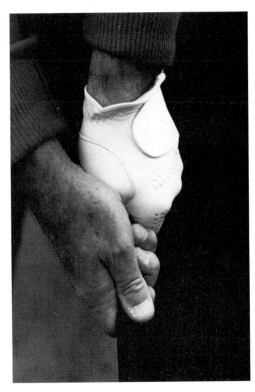

This strong grip—both hands rotated away from the target—will help you hit a draw shot.

release the clubface freely through the impact zone, would probably benefit from playing with a stronger grip. This means that for a right-handed player, both your hands will be turned farther to the right on the handle. As you look down, you should see three knuckles on your left hand, and your right hand should also be turned slightly more underneath the club so that the palm of your right hand matches or parallels the palm of your left.

Player C tees the ball up in the center of the teeing area, aims for a precise spot in the center of the fairway, keeps his grip pressure very light and tries to make a free-flowing swing. Unfortunately, he hits the ball on the heel of the clubface, so that the shot flies low and left of his intended line. The ball hits the tree guarding the left side of the fairway about 140 yards away, rattles around a bit and drops down in the rough. Fortunately, the ball has fallen just clear of the tree, on the fairway side, so he has a swing; but the ball is lying in tangled rough and he's a long way from the green.

You'd like to think if you hit a good fairway wood you could still get home in three. But this is no time for a heroic shot. Sometimes, it's actually good to draw a poor lie like you have here, because it takes the decision about gambling out of your hands. It's obvious that you have little choice but to play safe. If you think the longest club you can hit solidly from this rough is a 6-iron, do yourself a favor and hit a 7. Play the ball just back of center in your stance, with your hands well ahead of the clubhead and the clubface open, since the rough will tend to grab the club and close it down. Keep your weight favoring your left side and make a steep swing dominated by your arms, striving to contact the ball first.

Player C hits a solid shot with some extra run, advancing the ball 130 yards.

You're left with about 240 yards to the green, out of your range. You do, however, want to clear those fairway bunkers, which requires a carry of 150 yards. I think you're better off leaving a short pitch for your fourth, rather than laying your third way back where the B Player was in two. So, go with your 5-wood. Aim for the left center, allowing for some fade, and swing smoothly.

Player C makes fairly good contact and the ball lands in the center of the fairway, about 60 yards from the flag.

You have a slight downhill lie for your fourth shot, but the lie is good. Here, you should use your sand wedge rather than hitting a three-quarter pitching wedge as most higher-handicappers tend to do. Align yourself just slightly left of the flag, with the club's leading edge square to the hole. Play the ball off the center of your stance, with your hands about two inches in front of the ball. The key here is to simply try to make solid, downward contact. Never try to lift a sand-wedge pitch. You've taken the sand wedge because it supplies you with more loft to start with. Make a crisp, aggressive, three-quarter swing and keep your head still.

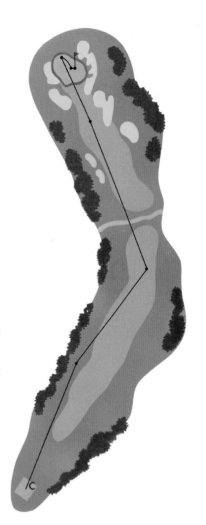

Player C executes this simple shot fairly well. However, because he's not advanced enough to impart backspin on the ball, it stops some 30 feet past the hole.

You still have a touchy putt to negotiate, downhill and with a little break to the right. Look at the putt from both sides of the hole, concentrating on a feel for the speed.

Player C hits the putt a little too softly, and it curls away to the right and pulls up just short. But he strokes the ball into the back of the cup, and scores a 6—which is really his own personal par. Not bad, when you consider he hit the tree with his tee shot.

COMMON STRATEGIC AND SHOT-MAKING ERRORS BY THE C PLAYER

- Gambling from trouble on long holes
- Scooping the ball with the wedges

Butch's Lessons

When you've gotten in trouble off the tee, there's an overwhelming urge to try to make up for the bad shot with a heroic recovery. Giving in to this urge is often what leads to the disaster hole, the 8 or 9 that ruins your round. Remember that whenever you've hit a bad shot, the important thing is to get your next shot back into a safe area. Always sacrifice distance and try to play a solid, safe second when you're in deep rough or trees—even when I'm not there to help you.

The loft of a normal sand wedge is about 56 degrees, while the lob wedge features 60 degrees. These are ample lofts to hit a high, soft shot, even when you deliver the ball a descending blow. Play basic pitch shots when you're in the 50- to 75-yard range, instead of trying to scoop the ball upward; you'll find you'll hit the green almost every time and land shots close to the cup more frequently.

HOLE	1	2	3	4	5	6	7	8	9	OUT	
YARDS	366	380	485	177	368	373	103	515	356	3123	
PAR	4	4	5	3	4	4	3	5	4	36	
Player A	5	5	5	3	3	4	3	5			
Player B	5	6	5	4	5	5	4	5			
Player C	6	4	8	4	5	5	5	6			

HOLE	10	11	12	13	14	15	16	17	18	IN	TOTAL
YARDS	183	508	121	339	339	417	407	452	510	3276	6399
PAR	3	5	3	4	4	4	4	4	5	36	72
Player A											
Player B											
Player C											

I n 1975, Hall Thompson founded Shoal Creek, a 7000-yard-plus golf course in Birmingham, Alabama, that he actually had a hand in creating with part-time course architect Jack Nicklaus. Nicklaus, along with Thompson, wanted to build a course that members would feel comfortable playing, but that was challenging enough to host a major championship. Their dreams came true.

In 1984, Shoal Creek was put to the test when the club hosted the PGA Championship. Because the fairways were fairly wide and the smooth fast greens receptive to iron shots, there were mostly rave reviews, particularly from the winner Lee Trevino, who shot 273 for four rounds, and runner-up Gary Player, who shot a course record 63 in the second round.

Nobody likes their course to be "eaten up" by the pros, so changes were made to the original layout, mostly to toughen it up. Tees were lengthened on par-3 holes 13 and 16. Trees were added to par-4 and par-5 holes, to put more of a premium on driving accuracy and to reduce the size of bailout areas near the green. Bunkers were moved closer to the green to bring them more into play. Not all changes made the course harder; for example, some greens were enlarged to better accommodate a long iron or fairway wood shot.

The next time the PGA was held at Shoal Creek was in 1990. Wayne Grady won the championship that year, and his winning score was 282, nine strokes higher than Trevino's 1984 score.

Today, Shoal Creek is recognized as a world-class course and is extremely enjoyable to play. Members think it's fun; the pros who visit think it's a great challenge.

The 9th hole measures a mere 356 yards, but it's not easy. First of all, it doglegs left, which is not something faders or slicers want to hear, particularly since two fairway traps down the right side are reachable from the tee. Second, the approach shot requires a carry over water, which is a quality common to many Nicklaus courses. If you miss the "drink," you'll probably land in one of the four sand traps. Even if you do hit the green in regulation, you'll still have to fight for par, since there are big breaks in the slick surface. On the tee: Player A.

Player A

If there is one hole that's shaped perfectly for your draw shot, this is it. If you wind the ball around the corner, you will be left with only a short iron into the green. A birdie is there for the taking.

Player A hits a wonderful tee shot around the corner of the dogleg. In fact, I'm surprised it finishes only 240 yards out. Instead of playing a straight second shot or a tiny fade into the fat of the green, he tries to get cute and hit a big left-to-right cut. His plan is to work the ball back to the pin, while avoiding the carry over water. His plan fails, because the ball flies dead straight, over the green, into the back left bunker. The ball is buried, so he really can't go for the hole without the risk of running the ball through the green and into the water. Instead, he aims at the fat portion of the green and hits a shot with a large degree of left-to-right spin. He's a little unlucky, because the ball rolls on after landing, but that could be expected. When the ball is buried, it will always come out hot, although imparting cut-spin on the ball will slow it. Player A stays cool, carefully lines up his putt, then sinks it for par.

COMMON STRATEGIC AND SHOTMAKING ERROR BY THE A PLAYER
- Not lining up correctly to hit a cut shot

Butch's Lessons

The next time you want to hit a big cut shot, aim the clubface differently and don't try to play the shot by feel.

You correctly aimed your feet, hips, and shoulders left of the target, in an open position. However, you aimed the clubface left of tar-

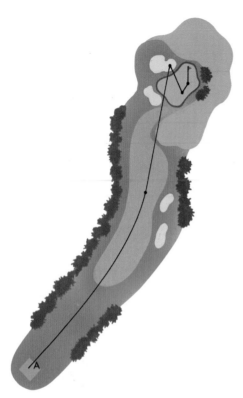

get also. You made a good backswing, but in swinging down you tried to hold the club open by delaying the release. Forget trying to hit the shot like that. Instead, aim the clubface at your "final" target, the pin. Then just swing normally. The ball will start its flight along your body line, then move toward the pin, where you aimed the clubface.

The B Player

Player B tries to hit a draw around the corner, just like the A player, but instead blocks the ball into the right rough, 206 yards off the tee, 150 yards from the green.

I commend you for your courage to try to hit a draw around the corner, just like Player A did. However, don't think with your heart, think with your head. In short, don't try a shot you don't know how to hit consistently at will.

After listening to my lecture, Player B starts thinking strategically. He positions the ball off his forward foot, and sets up open (feet, knees, hips, and shoulders aiming slightly more left of target), planning to hit a soft left-to-right fade. After setting the clubface perpendicular to an area of green left of the flag, he stares down the target, correctly forming a visual picture of the perfect shot in his mind's eye.

He makes a controlled compact backswing. Because of his setup position, he cuts across the ball slightly with a 6-iron, sending it flying along the precise line he imagined. He hits a wonderful shot, landing the ball 20 feet left of the flag. The fade was a smart shot to play, because it allowed him to go around much of the water and avoid the lurking traps guarding the right-hand pin-side of the green.

Player B takes great care in lining up his putt, but I notice that he is reaching too much for the ball. This setup promotes tension in the arms. In turn, tension prevents him from accelerating the putter through impact. That's the key reason he leaves the ball short of the hole.

Player B taps in for a well-earned par nevertheless.

COMMON STRATEGIC AND SHOTMAKING ERRORS BY THE B PLAYER

- Trying to hit a draw using a swing he's not familiar with
- Improperly setting up to putt

Butch's Lessons

The golf course is no place to experiment. It was obvious, from the way you pulled the club well to the inside, that you had heard or read that the secret to hitting a draw was employing a flat backswing action. This is true; a flatter backswing plane enhances the rotation of the forearm on the downswing, and encourages the clubface to turn over slightly through impact, with the toe of the club leading the heel. As a result, draw-spin is imparted on the ball.

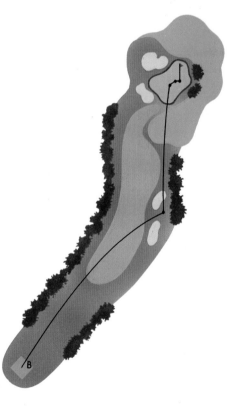

What you did wrong was consciously pulling the club inside, swinging it far behind your body. When the club swings on such an exaggerated inside path, it is virtually impossible to return it to a square impact position without rerouting it at the top or manipulating it with your hands on the downswing. The secret to promoting the proper slightly inside path is making sure that you turn your shoulders in a clockwise direction on the backswing, while keeping the hands quiet. When you do that, the club swings along an inside path all by itself, never entering the "danger zone" behind the body.

Let the turning action of the shoulders control the club's path. Don't pull the club inside with your hands.

In order to alleviate body tension, and ensure that you accelerate the putter through the ball, set up with your arms under your shoulder sockets. Letting the arms hang down naturally, rather than extending them outward, will keep you nice and relaxed at address. That way, you'll hit solid putts that reach the hole.

The C Player

The shot the C player hits—a 230-yard hook around the corner—shocks me. From the stunned and delighted look on his face,

I can see that it shocks him, too! This goes to show how just making a small change, such as strengthening the grip by rotating the hands away from the target, can change a player's swing plane and ball flight. The unfortunate thing: The ball lands in a bad lie in the rough, about 125 yards from the green.

For his approach shot, Player C maintains his exaggerated strong grip position, and again swings on an overly flat plane. This flat swing causes the club to hit more grass than ball; as a result, the clubface twists into a closed position, sending the ball flying into a sand bunker left of the green.

In deep rough, you want to take the club back quite steeply, and hit the ball as cleanly as possible with a powerful descending blow. Don't ever sweep the ball, or you'll be hacking around so much you'll be forced to put an "X" on your card. More on how to recover from this lie when I give you my post-hole lessons.

The lie in the bunker is slightly uphill, and the shot is relatively long, so Player C smartly opens the clubface much less than he would normally when playing a standard bunker shot from a flat lie. Unfortunately, he virtually stops the swing at impact; consequently, the ball falls some 12 feet short of the hole.

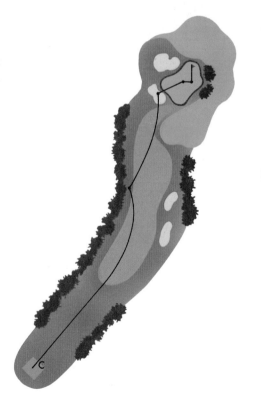

Concentrating intently over the putt, he makes a pure arms-shoulders stroke, knocking the ball dead into the back of the cup for a super par.

COMMON STRATEGIC AND SHOTMAKING ERRORS BY THE C PLAYER

- Experimenting on the course
- Using the wrong technique to hit out of deep rough

- Failing to follow through when hitting relatively long sand shots

Butch's Lessons

Switching to a stronger grip will definitely help you start shaping shots from right to left, rather than slicing them well right of target. Nevertheless, I will give you the same advice I gave the B player: Experiment with this grip in practice first, so that you learn to hit a controlled draw. Then, bring that shot to the course.

What's so interesting about grip changes is how they help you hit particular shots. Because you are far less experienced than the A player, you used that same new strong grip of yours to recover from deep rough. As a result, you swung the club on too flat a path, and hit a weak shot short of the green.

When the ball is sitting down in rough, it's critical that you swing the club on an upright plane.

When the ball is sitting down in rough, take a short or medium iron. Even the pros don't try to recover with a long iron. Also, revert back to your weaker grip for this shot. This type of hold helps promote a more upright swing. Allow your wrists to hinge on the backswing, and pull the club down hard into the back of the ball. You'll be surprised how far you hit the ball.

DRILL (FOR TRAINING YOURSELF TO HIT DOWN IN DEEP ROUGH)

To ingrain the correct feeling of swinging on an upright plane, and hitting down very sharply, practice playing shots off your right foot. The ball position will exaggerate the steepness of your swing, but that's the best way to acquaint yourself with the feeling of swinging on this type of plane.

You should always follow through on sand shots (unless you're hitting from a standard buried lie), but particularly when the ball is a fairly long distance from the hole. In your case, you were nearly 40 feet away; when facing this shot, be sure to accelerate your arms in the hitting area and swing up into a high finish.

HOLE	1	2	3	4	5	6	7	8	9	OUT	
YARDS	366	380	485	177	368	373	103	515	356	3123	
PAR	4	4	5	3	4	4	3	5	4	36	
Player A	5	5	5	3	3	4	3	5	4	37	
Player B	5	6	5	4	5	5	4	5	4	43	
Player C	6	4	8	4	5	5	5	6	4	47	
HOLE	10	11	12	13	14	15	16	17	18	IN	TOTAL
YARDS	183	508	121	339	339	417	407	452	510	3276	6399
PAR	3	5	3	4	4	4	4	4	5	36	72
Player A											
Player B											
Player C											

WINGED FOOT GOLF CLUB (WEST)
Par 3: 183 yards

Surely you haven't forgotten the 5th hole at Winged Foot's East Course that you played today. The West's 10th will be even more memorable, because as hole ratings go this one is a hell of a lot harder—and it's a par 3!

This "one-shotter" plays long from the middle tees, and demands that you hit the ball solidly to carry over a valley. It also demands pinpoint accuracy for your shot to avoid the two big bunkers set into the hillside, the additional two sand traps to the sides of the green, and the thick greenside rough that surrounds the putting surface. What's more, if you miss the hole long, you'll either face a treacherous downhill chip or be out of bounds.

Tillinghast, the course designer, considered this the best par-3 hole he ever built. When you consider that he created superb short holes on such wonderful challenging courses as Baltusrol in New Jersey, Somerset Hills in California, and Five Farms in Maryland, that's saying something special about "The Foot's" 10th.

When the United States Open was first played here in 1974, the West Course humbled the world's greatest players. Hale Irwin won with a 72-hole score of seven over par. Needless to say, many faltered at the par-3 10th. See how you can score.

The A Player

On some courses, such as Augusta National, the secret to scoring is keeping the ball below the hole on the greens. Here, the same principle applies because the green slopes severely from back to front. Even with your skill, you don't want to be left with a long putt or chip from behind the hole. I say that, because during the Opens that were contested here in 1974 and 1984, some players actually rolled off the front of the green with their first putt. Today, the surfaces aren't as slick as they were then, but still be careful. This is one time where I'd favor the club that will land you on the front portion of the green.

Player A selects a 4-iron, since that's his 185-yard club. However, he hits it very flush, landing it some 30 feet above the hole.

His approach putt surprises me because it actually stops short of the hole. He must have smartly visualized the hole being closer than it actually was. The mental image is designed to help enhance your ability to lag the ball short of the cup.

To say Player A holes out for a score of 3 is an understatement. He hits the ball so hard that it bangs into the back of the hole, pops up into the air, then luckily comes down into the cup.

COMMON STRATEGIC AND SHOTMAKING ERRORS BY THE A PLAYER
- Taking too much club for the situation
- Hitting short putts too hard

Butch's Lessons

It's hard for me to fault your fine tee shot. You employed a fine swing and the ball was struck solidly. However, I wish you would have chosen the 5-iron. When hitting this club, you normally carry the ball 175 yards, so if you struck it solidly and the ball didn't bounce forward at all once it landed on the green, you still would

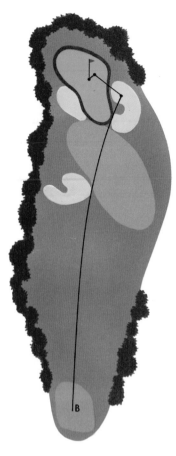

have faced only a 25-foot putt. If your tee shot spun back, fine; if you didn't catch the ball quite so solidly and it finished farther in front of the green, that's fine, too. You would have faced an uphill putt that would have allowed you to aggressively go for your birdie with no real fear of three-putting. For all the trouble lurking around the green, the critical factor for you on this hole is the back-to-front slope of the putting surface. Placing the ball above the hole is just asking for trouble, even when you've bypassed the traps and the treacherous fringe.

Speaking of "three-jabs," you were lucky that par putt dropped. I'm not against taking the break out of a putt by hitting the ball more solidly at medium pace. But hitting the ball as hard as you did is dangerous. If you would have missed the hole, the ball would have rolled off the green, and you would have been scrambling for double-bogey.

The B Player

Before Player B set up to the ball, I thought all he had to do was pick the right club, remember to aim left of the hole, and stay down with the shot.

When it comes time to play his shot, he does everything right except stay down. The result: a severe slice that sends the ball flying into the right greenside trap. From the trap, he plays a textbook sand shot, hitting the ball stiff to the hole. A nice "sandie" for par.

- Swinging too fast

Butch's Lessons

The 5-wood you chose was the perfect club. There was no need for you to swing so fast. You were right to say that you "stood up" at the start of the downswing, because in fact you did lose the flex in your knees. When you do this, it's virtually impossible to shift your weight correctly onto your left foot on the downswing, and rotate your hips through the ball. As a result, the clubface can't square up to the ball. Instead, it arrives in an open position, causing the ball to slice.

> ### DRILL (FOR SLOWING DOWN YOUR SWING ON WOOD SHOTS)
>
> Hit a 7-iron shot.
> Now, go through the entire bucket of balls, trying to hit your woods only as far as that 7-iron shot. You'll be surprised how this smooths out your quick tempo.

Player C

Player C cuts across the ball and hits a vicious slice into the thick rough near the green.

From there, he uses a pitching wedge for his short pitch to the green, but the ball comes out hot and goes flying over the green. Unlike on the 7th hole, however, where his poor chip resulted from a lot of wrist and hand action, Player C hits a beautiful chip back using the big muscles of the arms and shoulders in what looks very much like his putting technique, leaving himself an easy two-foot putt that he makes for bogey.

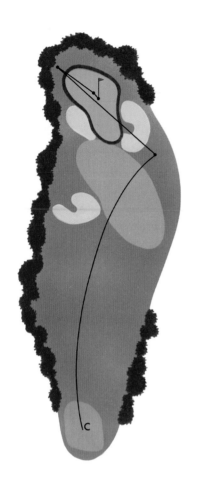

- Improper downswing action on the tee shot
- Bad choice of club and improper technique on second shot

Butch's Lessons

The reason you cut across the ball is that you came over the top on the downswing. You let your right shoulder jut outward instead of staying behind your left. The true cause of this common fault is not working the downswing properly. You must begin the downswing by "starting from the ground up," as my dad used to say. In your case, you like to let the left heel raise up on the backswing, so your first move down should be to replant that heel. Flat-footed players who come over the top should slide their hips laterally, rather than turn their hips in a counterclockwise direction. When the lower body leads, the hands, arms, shoulders, and club will follow. Only if the lower body is "dead" will the upper body want to take over.

On your second shot, the ball was sitting down slightly, yet you chose a pitching wedge. I know you like this club, but it's not what you needed to loft the ball over the sand trap and stop it relatively quickly. A much better choice would have been either a sand wedge or, better yet, the lob wedge that features 60 degrees of loft. Furthermore, you used a level, all-arms chip stroke. That worked fine on your chip that followed, but for this pitch you

do need to make a short wristy backswing like the one I'm using in the accompanying photograph. This will enhance your feel, plus allow you to drop the club down sharply into the grass behind the ball and pop it softly into the air.

In hitting a soft pitch out of rough, use a wristy backswing.

HOLE	1	2	3	4	5	6	7	8	9	OUT	
YARDS	366	380	485	177	368	373	103	515	356	3123	
PAR	4	4	5	3	4	4	3	5	4	36	
Player A	5	5	5	3	3	4	3	5	4	37	
Player B	5	6	5	4	5	5	4	5	4	43	
Player C	6	4	8	4	5	5	5	6	4	47	

HOLE	10	11	12	13	14	15	16	17	18	IN	TOTAL
YARDS	183	508	121	339	339	417	407	452	510	3276	6399
PAR	3	5	3	4	4	4	4	4	5	36	72
Player A	3										
Player B	3										
Player C	4										

There are very few golfers, either professional or amateur, who are neutral about golf courses designed solely by Pete Dye. It's impossible not to have a strong opinion—you either love them or hate them. Dye is perhaps golf architecture's staunchest defender of par; his harshest critics say he never wants *anyone* to make a par! Dye is world famous for his small, diabolically contoured greens, his many pot bunkers that combine with myriad man-made humps and mounds to guard the greens like fortresses, his railroad ties and his vast waste bunkers, and his many blind shots from both tee and fairway. If you prefer to play your golf on courses that are relatively straightforward and predictable, give a wide berth to Pete Dye's courses. If, on the other hand, you relish the challenge of trying your hand on truly demanding layouts, you can't do much better than to play a Pete Dye course. And if you're playing a Pete Dye course, you can't do much better than to try the Tournament Players Club in Ponte Vedra, Florida, site of the PGA Tour's annual Players Championship.

You could probably argue that there are 18 great holes on this golf course. In my opinion, though, you can't beat the par-5 11th as one of the supreme strategic par 5s in the world. It is literally a "chessboard built on grass"—there is a limitless variety of ways to attack this golf hole. And you can make anything on it, from an eagle on up to—well, you know what I mean.

The 11th at the Tournament Players Club is a twisting, serpentine type of hole, effectively playing as a double-dogleg. For starters, you must thread your drive between stands of tall pine trees on both sides. Farther down on the left is a sandy waste area that could also prove bothersome to the long hitters.

The fun really starts on the second shot, which traverses the middle area of the hole which doglegs fairly to the left. This section of the hole is bisected by a tongue of the large pond that continues around to the right of the hole. It is also bisected by a segment of the huge waste bunker that also continues down the right side of the fairway and then all the way around the green. A narrow, difficult-to-hit slice of fairway lies beyond these hazards and bends back slightly to the right for the remaining 120 yards or so to the green.

Thus, depending on the length and positioning of the drive, the golfer will have three choices for the second shot. For the long knocker who has hit a big tee shot with a draw down the left side to shorten the hole, a temptation will beckon to go for the green in two. For most players who have hit a good drive, however, the most likely choice of shot will be a second shot to the left-side fairway area. The golfer who has either hit a shorter drive or missed the fairway into trouble will have to lay up the second shot short of the dogleg that contains both the water and waste area, leaving a longer third from a difficult angle.

The green is at least 40 yards deep, so it is possible to hit either a high or a low shot into it. However, the green is only about half as wide as it is long, and it is set to the right of that last fairway area, so that it is a semipeninsula whose entire front, right, and rear are ringed by the waste area that started back down the fairway. To the left is a nest of three pot bunkers mixed with several small but steep mounds that spell at least "bogey" for anyone who pulls the approach shot even a trifle. Add another pot bunker just in front of

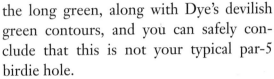

the long green, along with Dye's devilish green contours, and you can safely conclude that this is not your typical par-5 birdie hole.

I believe this is a world-class hole because it calls for precise execution of a well-thought-out game plan. Let's turn our attention to how each level of player can make the best possible score at the TPC's 11th.

The A Player

Despite the fact that I've painted you a picture of what might be considered a real hell hole, I also think that this is a hole where you must take an aggressive approach from the tee. The reason goes back to the three options I mentioned that players may face on their second shot. The most desirable option, of course, is to drive to where you can take out your 3-wood and have a go at the green in two. If you are capable of hitting your driver at least 250 yards with a good swing, you should hit it off the tee, because you'll need every inch to have any shot at the green. In addition, although no tee shot at the Tournament Players Club could be called easy, you do have about 40 yards of fairway between the tree lines here. So definitely take out the big club and give it your best swing. Even if you can't get home in two, you want good length off the tee. That way, you can at least hit your second over the water and sand, and set yourself up for a relatively easy third shot. This is a hole where playing too safe off the tee might turn out to be more dangerous than hitting a driver.

Your goal is to start a driver down the right side, and turn it over from right to left so that it works back to the center or left side of the fairway with plenty of roll. Here's a tip to help you get this result: On the backswing, make a conscious effort to move your left knee to the right, so that you work it inward and behind the ball at the top of your backswing. This move does two things for you: It gets your lower body weight loaded behind the ball, so that you can deliver more power through impact; also, working the knee to the right (rather than having it piston forward, toward the ball) aids you in making a backswing on a more rounded, flatter plane, so that you can more easily impart right-to-left draw-spin to the ball.

Player A makes a good, aggressive swing and drills a good drive down the right side with a draw. He hit the ball 250 yards, but it ends up a little right of center, so he hasn't cut any distance off the hole.

You've got your hand on that wood, so I gather you'd like to take a rip at the green. From this angle you'd have to hit the ball around 250 yards to carry the water. All things considered, this is a shot that only Tiger Woods should think about going for. The correct shot for you is option two—the lay-up to the left that will hopefully set you up for a simple third shot and a good birdie try.

Just because you have decided to lay up, though, doesn't mean you have a shot that you can go to sleep on. As I mentioned earlier, the area of fairway to the left is none too wide. Leak it right and you'll be in the waste bunker; pull it left and there are more trees and rough. Think about the distance you'd like to leave yourself for your easiest possible third shot. If you'd like to get it within 90

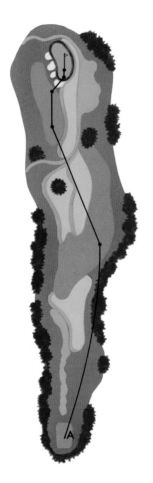

yards for a nice sand-wedge shot, that means you'll probably need to hit your lay-up about 170 to 175 yards with perhaps a 5-iron. To help you play this shot well, imagine that *your lay-up shot is actually a shot to a par-3 hole.* You want to hit this shot as precisely as any other. That's one of the things that is so tough about this hole—you can't bail out on any shot, including the lay-up second.

Player A hits a solid second shot exactly where he wants to, in the fairway and 90 yards from the middle of the green.

Before you automatically grab your sand wedge, take a good look at the pin position. Is it well up front, or way back? Either extremity could add or subtract 10 to 12 yards from your base yardage, so know exactly where that flag is. Secondly, keep in mind that the pin position might alter the type of pitch you play. If it's up front, like we'll pretend it is today, you should subtract 10 yards from your total distance (i.e., 90 – 10 = 80) and definitely play a lofted sand-wedge shot. If the pin were back, you'd be wise to consider playing a controlled, lower shot with a pitching wedge, letting it land in the front to middle of the green before releasing toward the hole. It's rarely a good strategy to try to loft a high, floating shot all the way to a pin on the back. This is particularly true here since the back of this green is formed into a small "deck," and it falls off into the waste bunker which works its way around the back of the putting surface.

When playing the high sand-wedge shot, remember to open the clubface and accelerate the club faster in the impact zone. Otherwise you'll fall short of the green.

Unfortunately, Player A decelerates in the impact zone, and peeks, so the ball comes up short of the green. However, from there, he makes an excellent up and down for par.

COMMON STRATEGIC AND SHOTMAKING ERRORS BY THE A PLAYER

- Thinking about going for the green, when a perfect shot is required
- Decelerating on short pitch shots

Butch's Lessons

Most A players will get into trouble after a good drive because taking a whack at the green, even if it's an unrealistic shot, is too tantalizing to pass up. But unless you execute a long fairway wood to perfection, too many things can go wrong. So, unless the lie and conditions (wind, etc.) are ideal, and you are absolutely sure you can comfortably reach the green with your fairway wood, put that club away and take out an iron that will put you in position for a good pitch to the pin.

To cure your problems of peeking and decelerating on short pitch shots, try looking at the front of the ball. This mental gimmick will help you accelerate through the ball, and hit shots to the pin.

The B Player

For the player in the 10- to 16-handicap range, this is an excellent par-5 that requires three solid shots in order to get onto the putting surface in regulation. If you are a golfer who hits the ball a little shorter on average than the A player, again, this is a tee shot that calls for an aggressive play with the driver. You need to get reasonable distance off the tee, at least the 225 to 230 yards you get with good contact, in order to get a clear look at the landing area to the left and have a distance to it that is well within your range.

So, go with your driver, but keep the thought in mind that you want to stay *smooth*. Resist the temptation to hit the ball harder

When playing a punch shot, try to put the club in the toe-up follow-through position.

than you know how and just try to swing the club smoothly and levelly through impact.

Player B swings a trifle fast, but sends the ball 230 yards and keeps it on the short grass. He's now in a good position to try to put the ball into nearly the same position as the A player. Of course, he is 20 yards farther back in the fairway, so he would have to hit his second shot that much farther, say 200 yards, to get there. My thinking here is that he not try to get quite that far up the fairway with a 3-wood unless he's extremely confident of his accuracy with that club. Instead, he should go with a more lofted 5-wood, and play the shot with all the care he would use on a longer par-3 hole—picking a landing spot carefully and making sure both the clubface and his body are accurately aligned to it.

He takes my advice and it pays off. Player B hits the 5-wood down the fairway 190 yards, and is now left with a shot of about 100 yards to the flag, positioned in the front portion of the green.

Because the wind is in Player B's face, I advise him to play a punch shot with a 9-iron. Here's how he should execute it.

First, address the ball from a narrow stance, with the ball positioned just back of center or off the inside of your right heel. Keep most of your weight at address on your left foot. Make a compact swing controlled with your arms, so that you shift less weight back and forward during the swing than you normally would. On the downswing, pull the club firmly down and through the ball, with an abbreviated follow-through in which you finish *pointing the club toward the target.* The shot will start off much lower than a normal pitch, and will take one or two skips upon landing, but then, if you've struck it cleanly, it will check up. In the wind, this shot is much easier to control than a high pitch shot.

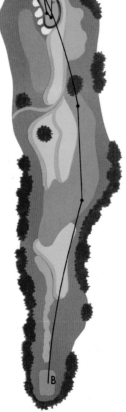

Player B hits the ball on target, but a little strong. Still, he manages to two-putt for par from the back of the green.

COMMON STRATEGIC AND SHOTMAKING ERRORS BY THE B PLAYER
- Trying to overpower the tee shot
- Hitting punch shots too far

Butch's Lessons

Just because you have decided to hit a driver, it doesn't mean you have to try to pound the ball. Swinging beyond your capabilities with the driver is probably the biggest cause of wasted strokes in golf. Start thinking of your driver as you would any club—as a club you want to put your best swing on, rather than a separate entity from everything else in your bag that you need swing harder with. Try to make your smoothest, best-balanced swing with your driver, and you'll find yourself hitting far fewer shots that put you in jail.

Practice your punched approach shots with your short irons and wedges. By taking a lot of extraneous body movement out of these shots and delivering a controlled, downward blow, you'll find yourself getting the ball closer to the hole, especially in windy conditions.

The C Player

The hole you have to play is a slightly different one from the one your playing partners have played. For reasons I'll discuss at length in the "Lessons" section, I believe you should think of the 11th at TPC as a "par 6." You would have to hit three perfect shots to reach the green in what the scorecard says is regulation, but the design of this hole allows you a chance to play a series of stress-free shots that will hopefully leave you with a putt for a par—a "birdie" on your "par 6." Understanding your own game is the crucial step toward improving your scores.

For starters, you should take a different strategy from the tee: hit the club you're most confident with off the tee. If that's a 3-wood, fine. If it's a 5-wood, you should hit that. You simply want to make a relaxed swing and put the ball in play.

Player C hits a higher 5-wood shot than he planned, but it lands on a hard area of fairway and comes to rest 180 yards from the tee.

You can play this comfortable shot off the tee because you've already made your decision about your second shot—you're not going to try to hit the ball over the hazards to that left-side fairway, as your playing partners did. Instead, you're going to lay up short of the waste area and the water. In this situation, or a similar one, check your yardage carefully to the end of the "first" fairway area. If you have 170 yards to the end of the fairway, pick a club that will leave you 15 yards short of that, probably no more than a 5-iron. Again, aim your second shot just as you would to a par 3 with a small green. By keeping your shot demands simple, the chances are increased that you'll keep the ball in the fairway.

Player C hits a nice lay-up shot to within 175 yards of the green.

With such a narrow target to hit, you must now play it smart and lay up short of that bunker in front of the green, rather than trying to hit a "career" 3-iron. To accomplish this goal, you must know how far it is to keep the ball short of that bunker and in the fairway, and select a club that you *can't* reach the bunker with. This will probably be a 6- or 7-iron.

Player C hits the perfect third shot, to within 50 yards of the flag. However, in trying to scoop the ball into the air, he hits his fourth shot fat. From a position short of the green, he hits a wonderful soft pitch, then putts the ball in for a score of 6.

COMMON STRATEGIC AND SHOTMAKING ERRORS BY THE C PLAYER

- Hitting a 5-wood too high
- Chili-dipping your pitch to the green

Butch's Lessons

Before helping you improve your shotmaking skills, I do want you to understand the strategic side of golf, and how playing sensibly helped you score a bogey and avoid disaster on a very tough hole.

Many C players are under the impression that thinking strategically is something only A players do. This is very far from the truth. Playing smart golf is even more important for C players, because they lack the shotmaking skills to score birdies and make up for a bad hole. In your case, if you try to be a hero and hit shots that are not in your bag right now, playing risky golf and taking chances—treating the game as a lottery—you will have more bad days than good days.

Your objective is to keep high scores off your card, especially the score of 8, or what's commonly called the dreaded "snowman."

There's nothing wrong with trying to hit a long drive or a pro-type finesse shot, provided that you've first worked on these shots in practice. Too many high-handicappers try to play miracle shots, which explains why the words "if" and "should" come so frequently into their conversation at the 19th hole. If you are truly serious about lowering your handicap, you should only play shots you know you're capable of hitting. Don't try to carry the ball over a lake 230 yards away, for example, when you know in your heart you'd have to hit a miracle shot. Don't try to smash a long iron, or even a utility wood, all the way to the green from long rough, when you know in your heart that the odds are against you and the sensible play is to pitch out. The bottom line is: the sooner you mature as a player and start thinking strategically, the sooner you will lower your handicap. You will have more fun, too, planning out your shots and using your head as you would playing chess.

Good course strategists, such as Jack Nicklaus, are artists who know exactly how far they hit each club in their bag; how far the ball flies in the air, then rolls, on chip shots; how the ball reacts in different types of sand; and much more. The first smart thing you should do is go to the driving range, or out on the course in the early evening during the summer, and determine the average distance you hit the ball with a variety of clubs. (Not your best, your average.) This knowledge will allow you to place shots with pinpoint accuracy, so that you can put the ball in Position A, relative to your own skill, time after time. Play smartly and you'll be the one laughing to the bank with your winnings from Nassau bets.

Now, let me tell you how to hit the ball off the tee with a lower trajectory and improve your pitching skills.

When you exaggerate the lateral action of the lower body on the downswing, and flip your right hand under your left, you hit the ball extra high. To help you groove a level swing through impact and hit the ball on a more penetrating trajectory, work on these two drills:

DRILL 1

Assume your address position but put the thumb of your left hand in your left pants pocket. Now pull on the pocket so you encourage your hip to rotate or "clear" to the left of target. You need this type of rotation to return the club squarely and powerfully to the ball.

DRILL 2

Imagine there's a second ball a couple of inches in front of the "real" one. Swing, trying to hit the imaginary ball. This mental image will promote a more extended release of your arms, thereby preventing the right hand from turning under your left one.

Many amateur players hit short pitch shots "fat" because of poor mechanics. Never try to "scoop" the ball up on pitch shots, but give it a crisp, descending blow instead. Your sand wedge has plenty of loft to get the ball nicely into the air when you hit down on it. Address the ball in the center of your stance with your hands about two inches ahead. Swing back to the halfway point, then down and through with your arms. Also, you may want to heed the tip I gave Player A: look at the *front* of the ball to ensure you hit through it.

HOLE	1	2	3	4	5	6	7	8	9	OUT	
YARDS	366	380	485	177	368	373	103	515	356	3123	
PAR	4	4	5	3	4	4	3	5	4	36	
Player A	5	5	5	3	3	4	3	5	4	37	
Player B	5	6	5	4	5	5	4	5	4	43	
Player C	6	4	8	4	5	5	5	6	4	47	
HOLE	10	11	12	13	14	15	16	17	18	IN	TOTAL
YARDS	183	508	121	339	339	417	407	452	510	3276	6399
PAR	3	5	3	4	4	4	4	4	5	36	72
Player A	3	5									
Player B	3	5									
Player C	4	6									

Welcome to what Jack Nicklaus, a six-time winner of the Masters championship, calls "the toughest par-3 tournament hole in golf." Despite its beauty and modest length, Augusta's 12th, called "Golden Bell," is a tricky, fickle, capricious beast. It is a hole where literally anything can happen, and indeed has during the 60-plus years that the Masters has been contested.

In 1980, Tom Weiskopf once took a 13 on this beautiful little monster, and claims he was trying on every shot. Tom Watson's bid to win a third Masters, in 1991, was derailed here once when his tee shot leaked into Rae's Creek, which lurks on the lip of the green. And, of course, Greg Norman lost the lead for good to Nick Faldo when he dunked his ball in the drink fronting the green and took a double-bogey 5.

Augusta's 12th has not elicited disaster from everyone, however. In 1958, a youthful Arnold Palmer displayed a cool head when he hit his tee shot into the bank behind the green and the ball embedded. Told he must play the ball as it lay, Palmer scored a 4 on the hole. However, because he felt he was entitled to drop his ball out of its own pitch mark, he then went back and played a provisional ball, taking the drop and making par; when the ruling was eventually made in his favor, Palmer won his first Masters by a single stroke. Many years later, another player won his first green jacket owing to a different kind of break, here at number 12. Fred Couples' slightly pushed tee shot in 1992 seemingly defied gravity by hugging the side of a bank instead of dropping back into the water. Couples' coup was complete when he deftly lobbed a wedge shot to within a foot of the hole and saved a precious par.

There are a number of factors that cause players such as Gary Player to call the 12th "the toughest par-3 in the world."

The green is approximately 100 feet long, yet at its shallowest point it is only 28 feet wide. The wind swirls most every day. Two big bunkers guard the back of the green. Water and a third bunker guard the front.

Today, the hole is placed in what is called the "sucker" position—on the right-center portion of the green, behind the bunker fronting the green. Play away, gentlemen.

Player A

Player A usually has no trouble hitting a fade. Here, however, he has to be careful not to come over the top and pull the ball dead left, or hold back his releasing action so long that he fades the ball too much and hits the ball into the water. Club selection is critical, too; not only does he have to select a stronger club to compensate for the fade, he must take the wind into consideration. But even that's not as easy as it sounds. There are times when the shot is actually downwind, but the flag on 12 is blowing toward you. That's because of the backdrop of trees behind the green; they can affect the wind just enough to change the way the flag is blowing, but have no real impact on the shot. As a result, most players at the Masters have learned the trick that Ben Hogan taught my father: On the 12th tee, look back at the flag on the 11th green. That's the wind direction you can believe for your crucial little tee shot here.

Today, the wind is blowing from left to right, so Player A has to keep in mind to aim farther left than normal. He smartly chooses a 9-iron, lays his ball on the ground, and very carefully goes through his preswing routine. He even takes an extra practice swing to make certain he has the feel of the action needed. His care is rewarded.

The ball starts out left of the back rear bunker, then fades toward the flag, landing practically pin-high 20 feet away.

He read the left-to-right putt correctly, but leaves his approach putt 5 feet short. From there, he holes out for a par 3.

COMMON STRATEGIC AND SHOTMAKING ERRORS BY THE A PLAYER

- Not using a tee
- Leaving his approach putt well short of the cup

Butch's Lessons

I realize that Lee Trevino believes you should not use a tee on par-3 holes. His thinking: You are so accustomed to playing shots with irons off the fairway without a tee, so why use one when playing par-3 holes?

Trevino is a special breed. The majority of pros use a tee because it prevents blades of grass from getting between the clubface and ball at impact. When this happens, the ball usually flies about 20 yards farther than normal. With a tee you get a clean hit, and control your distance better.

Yes, you did a good job of controlling your shot, but that was because the wind held your shot up. If there was no wind, the ball may have finished over the green. Trust me, use a tee.

When you face a breaking putt that's slightly downhill, give yourself a chance of knocking the birdie putt into the hole. If you go by the hole, a couple of feet or so, that's okay. You'll face an uphill putt coming back; these putts are much easier to hole than downhill sliders.

The B Player

Player B, fresh off a par on number 11, foolishly aims for the "sucker pin" located in the right-hand area of the 12th green. What's worse, he makes too short a swing with a 7-iron, never really completing his turn, not generating enough power to propel the ball all the way to the green. Luckily, the ball stays out of Rae's Creek. Still, it comes to rest on the grassy bank to the side of the sand trap fronting the green, leaving Player B a 10-yard shot off a relatively steep uphill lie.

To promote a high, soft-landing shot, Player B selects a lofted wedge, and plays the ball off his left instep. To encourage a freer arm swing, he assumes an open stance. He makes a short wristless backswing, like the one most pros recommend. On the downswing, he swings up the slope, keeping the clubface pointing at the sky through impact. The shot floats softly into the air, practically stops dead on the green, and comes to rest close enough to the hole to set up an easy one-putt conversion. What a great lob!

COMMON STRATEGIC AND SHOTMAKING ERRORS BY THE B PLAYER

- Making an overly compact swing
- Attacking a "sucker" pin

A compact iron swing is okay, as long as you remember to make a fairly strong shoulder turn.

Butch's Lessons

I'm glad to see you striving to make a compact swing on iron shots. Most pros shorten the backswing when playing short and medium irons, so that there's no chance of the wrists overcocking at the top of the swing. They also realize there's no need to create an extra-wide arc when they are hitting a control shot into a par 3.

The reason you hit the ball weak and right is that your swing was so short that you failed to make a strong enough turn. You need to turn the shoulders to create enough power to hit the ball your usual distance with a particular club. The clockwise winding action of the shoulders also directs the club on a shallower path, setting you in position for a clean hit at impact. When you fail to wind the shoulders at least 80 degrees, the club tends to swing on an overly steep plane. That type of backswing action causes you to hit down too abruptly on the ball, with the ball flying right of target.

DRILL (TO PROMOTE A BIGGER BACKSWING TURN)

As you practice hitting shots, try to turn your left shoulder past the ball. If you have trouble, allow your left heel to lift off the ground. If that doesn't work, swing a weighted club or a broom, so that you stretch your muscles.

You could have gotten away with your faulty swing had you aimed left of the flag, and probably faced a birdie putt, albeit a long one. But you aimed at the "sucker" pin and could have paid a dear price and scored double-bogey or worse. Next time you probably won't be so lucky, so start disciplining yourself to play safe in "sucker" pin situations.

The C Player

The C Player smartly plays for his slice, aiming ten yards left of the green. The ball lands on the far left-hand side of the green, some 60 feet from the hole. Actually, he is a little unlucky that the

Allowing your right wrist to hinge slightly will enhance your distance control on long putts.

wind doesn't blow his ball closer to the hole.

Facing a left-to-right breaking putt, Player C leaves his first putt very short, so it's no surprise that he finishes with a bogey 4.

COMMON STRATEGIC AND SHOTMAKING ERROR BY THE C PLAYER

- Using a wristless stroke on long putts

Butch's Lessons

I was pleased with your tee shot. As to your three-putt, it was caused by a poor lag putt from about 60 feet.

I know that you normally employ a wristless pendulum stroke. I'm all for that, when you face a short- or medium-length putt. In these instances, direction control is your priority. On long putts, however, distance control—hitting the ball at the proper pace—is all-important. To encourage good feel for the putterhead and distance, allow your right wrist to hinge slightly on the backswing.

HOLE	1	2	3	4	5	6	7	8	9	OUT	
YARDS	366	380	485	177	368	373	103	515	356	3123	
PAR	4	4	5	3	4	4	3	5	4	36	
Player A	5	5	5	3	3	4	3	5	4	37	
Player B	5	6	5	4	5	5	4	5	4	43	
Player C	6	4	8	4	5	5	5	6	4	47	
HOLE	10	11	12	13	14	15	16	17	18	IN	TOTAL
YARDS	183	508	121	339	339	417	407	452	510	3276	6399
PAR	3	5	3	4	4	4	4	4	5	36	72
Player A	3	5	3								
Player B	3	5	3								
Player C	4	6	4								

After you have survived the 12th at Augusta and some of the other holes I've thrown at you, you deserve a bit of a breather. The 13th hole on our course is from the Atlanta Athletic Club, the site of the 1976 U.S. Open. There, a 22-year-old Jerry Pate defied the odds by rallying from behind to score a three-under par 277, claiming the Open title by two strokes over Tom Weiskopf and Al Geiberger. One of golf's most famous shots is the miraculous 5-iron

Pate hit from the rough on the long, water-guarded 18th hole, to within two feet of the hole for the clinching birdie. Unfortunately, and largely due to injuries incurred a few years later, Pate's competitive career never matched his early promise, and that U.S. Open proved to be his brightest moment.

But back to number 13. This hole plays at a moderate 387 yards from the tournament tees, but from the members' markers it is a shorty at only 339 yards. Thus, for all three levels of player, distance will not be the problem. The main difficulties of the hole are that it's a severe dogleg to the right, and the hole is heavily wooded from tee to green.

From the tee, you have no sight of the green. The fairway makes its sharp turn to the right approximately 180 to 200 yards from the members' markers. All three levels of player can get around the corner. However, in addition to the trees that line the medium-width fairway, there is a big bunker guarding the right or inside corner of the dogleg. Obviously, you'd rather be in the fairway than in the bunker, but the closer you can put the ball to that bunker, the better your angle will be for the short iron shot into the green. That's because the green itself is guarded by a huge, sprawling bunker at its front left. Depending on where the hole is cut, shots hit from the far left, the safer side of the fairway, will sometimes have to take a tough line over that big greenside bunker and will also be a little longer. The design of the 13th at Atlanta A.C. follows a sound strategic principle: The nearer you dare to put your tee shot to trouble, the easier your approach shot will be; the safer you play the drive, the proportionately harder your second shot will be.

The medium-sized, bent-grass green is fairly quick and slopes pretty steeply down from back to front. So another key is to keep your approach below the hole. You're better off here with a 20-foot uphill birdie putt than with a 12-footer straight downhill, since you will be able to be much more aggressive with any uphill effort.

Let's see how each player should attack the hole.

The A Player

A lot of power hitters take out a driver and try to bomb it over the fairway bunker and some trees that guard the right side. If you decide on this strategy, be prepared to pay a severe price if you fail. Should you succeed you'll face a wedge shot of only 60 yards. This is fine, assuming you can handle "partial" wedge shots at least as well as full ones. Many golfers find they can actually get the ball closer to the hole from 110 yards or so than from half that distance. So how much have you gained?

By blasting a driver over the trees I think you take an unnecessary risk. If you lay up off the tee, you pretty well eliminate the chance of hitting the ball into the woods. The lay-up is likely to put you in range for a full pitching wedge, or at most a 9-iron to the green. So I believe you give yourself the best overall chance for a good score on this hole if you gear down and leave the driver in the bag.

You want to hit the ball about 210 or 215 yards, so depending on conditions a 2-iron is a likely choice. As a good player, your line should be down the right center of the fairway. This will give you the best possible angle to the flag, and also shorten the hole a bit. With the pin at center depth, you'd have about 120 yards left and could play an aggressive shot to the flag.

If you pull your long iron to the left side of the fairway, you're still in good shape. You'd have a shot that's a little longer and your angle to the pin wouldn't be as good, but birdie would still be a possibility. But what if you push your 2-iron into the bunker, you ask? Well, you don't want to do this. However, there's a relatively low lip on the bunker, so with the 9-iron or so you'd have remaining, you'd still be capable of hitting a shot close to the hole.

Player A hits a 2-iron solidly, but pulls the shot just a touch, so the ball ends up in the middle of the fairway rather than the right side.

You're no more than 125 yards from the flag, which as you can see is a little left of center on the green. You'll have to come over the bunker, but you've got plenty of green to work with. Remember, on this approach you want to keep the ball below the hole if possible. If you have any doubt about whether to hit a firm pitching wedge or a smooth 9-iron, in this case I'd say go with the pitching wedge. As an accomplished player, you might want to aim a few feet right of the hole and put a touch of right-to-left draw-spin on the

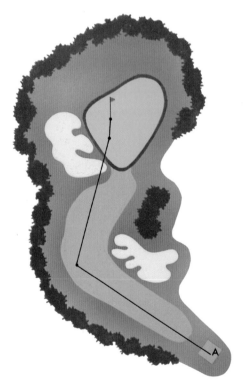

shot so that it will kick left and forward upon landing, to help you get it close. To achieve this result, play the ball one ball-width back in your stance from normal, and make a compact but aggressive swing, releasing fully through impact.

Player A's execution this time is close to perfect. The ball arches beautifully, lands nearly pin high 10 feet to the right of the hole, and the backspin and draw-spin cause it to kick left and then suck back, so that it finishes directly under the hole and 10 feet away.

Don't look for much break in your birdie putt. The putt

will be fairly slow owing to the upslope of the green. Get a clear picture of the ball rolling straight into the back of the cup. Then set up carefully and make a decisive stroke.

Player A hits the putt a little firmly, but the line is so dead center that it smacks the back of the cup and drops in. He's played the hole intelligently and executed almost flawlessly to earn a birdie 3.

COMMON STRATEGIC AND SHOTMAKING ERRORS BY THE A PLAYER

- Trying to cut the dogleg corner on a short par 4
- Hitting short-iron approaches past the hole

Butch's Lessons

You played the hole more like a pro than an amateur. While you didn't need them here, I would still like to offer some tips that I think will help you when playing short par-4 holes with sloping greens.

Unless a par-4 hole is so short (or you hit the ball so long) that you think you can nearly drive the green, it's usually not worth the gamble to hit your driver. If the only reward is to have a half- to three-quarter wedge shot as opposed to a full wedge in, the reward is not worth the risk if the shot must flirt with either heavy woods, water, or out of bounds. Besides, even the pros prefer a full wedge shot over a finessed wedge shot.

Often, on short approach shots, the good player will be unsure what club to hit, will go with the longer club, then will hit a great-looking shot that ends up 20 to 30 feet long. Then the player has a tough downhill putt that he or she can't really take a run at. If the greens are sloped from back to front, and especially if they are fast, lean toward taking the shorter club so that, if anything, you keep the ball short of the hole—or the green. Hitting the green in regulation should not always be your priority. When the pin is on the lower tier it's sometimes easier to feed the ball to the hole with a chip shot from in front of the green, and score par, than to putt downhill from the upper tier.

The B Player

Your strategy for the tee shot at number 13 will vary just a little from the A player's. You too would like to hit the ball 210 to 215 yards to put it past the corner and into easy range of the green. For you, however, this distance will probably require a 3-wood as opposed to a long iron for the stronger hitter. You can't expect to be as accurate as the A player, especially when you're hitting a wood and the A player hit an iron. Also, while it's possible for you to hit the green from that fairway bunker on the corner of the dogleg, it's something you'd probably want to avoid even more than the A player. Taking all that into account, your target should be slightly farther left—that is, the dead center of the fairway.

Tee the ball up only about a quarter to one-half inch, just a touch higher than you would for an iron shot on a par 3. Keep the swing compact and smooth.

Player B aims slightly right of his target and fails to make his best contact here—he contacts the ball toward the heel. The shot starts low and bends more to the right, flying perhaps 10 yards shorter than his normal hit. Still, because he planned the shot pretty well, the ball came to rest in the fairway, leaving him a perfect angle to the pin from the right side of the fairway.

Your shot will be about 135 to the hole, which translates to a 7- or an 8-iron shot. A birdie beckons. Before you go firing at the flag, though, just remember that you'd rather be putting from below the hole, and that if anything you should shade your shot to the right of the hole.

He decides to go with the 8-iron and hits it fairly well, but leaves the clubface a touch open. The ball lands on the front-right of the green rather than the center as he had planned, leaving him a putt of 35 feet uphill and with a right-to-left break. Not an easy putt, but fortunately the green is not lightning quick, like it was in the 1976 Open, so it's a little easier to judge the correct speed.

He gives it a nice stroke, hits the ball solidly, and it looks good most of the way. However, it loses its speed a little sooner than he thought it would, so that it dies short of the hole.

His second putt is uphill and also turns a hair left—the softer he hits it, the more it will break.

This is the type of putt where it pays to be decisive. Aim just right of center of the hole, playing for about a half-inch break, and stroke firmly. You'll make a far greater percentage by limiting the break on short putts and hitting them firmly, than by trying to curl them in.

Player B makes no mistake, rapping it right into the center of the hole, and saunters away with a solid par 4.

COMMON STRATEGIC AND SHOTMAKING ERRORS BY THE B PLAYER

- Not selecting the right line from the tee
- Heel hits off the tee and blocked irons

Butch's Lessons

Most golfers play dogleg holes too close to the dogleg, trying to shorten the hole. This is dangerous, especially on dogleg right holes, since most amateurs tend to fade their shots. Give the dogleg a wider berth, particularly if there is a bunker as well as a tree line to avoid. By aiming far enough left, toward the "safe" side of the fairway, even if you miss the shot slightly, you can end up in perfect position.

The chief cause of the problems you have, hitting woods off the heel and blocking irons, is consciously trying to pull the club down into a shallower downswing slot. The reason I know this: Once you reach the top your right elbow is shoved into your right hip. Don't force the club into a shallower downswing path by using a violent pulling action of the hands. Let your lower body lead the downswing, and the arms, hands, and club will follow. Furthermore, once the left hip clears, the sweet spot of the club, rather than the heel, will head for the back center portion of the ball.

DRILL (CURE FOR HITTING SHOTS OFF THE CLUB'S HEEL)

Practice hitting shots off sidehill lies (ball above feet). This will cause the toe of the club to lead its heel through impact, and train you to swing on an inside-square-inside path rather than an inside-to-outside path.

The C Player

For you, the strategy off the tee will be a little different. You need to hit the ball at least 180 yards to get a clear view of the green. You average about 190 with your 3-wood; however, you are less consistent in terms of distance (as well as accuracy) than either the A or B player. If you either pop your tee shot up or hit it thin, it may not get you far enough to have a clear shot to the green. For this reason I recommend you use a driver. If you hit it your normal 210 yards, the ball won't go through the fairway as a driver would for the longer hitters. And if you mishit it a little, it may still go far enough to give you a look at the green.

Your alignment should be a little different, too. Since a slice is your most common mistake, you've got to allow more for that possibility. Align your body and the clubhead toward the fairway's left edge so that your normal fade will bring the ball back to the left-center, which should be your ultimate target area. If you hit the shot as planned, you'll be a little farther from the green than the A and B players and your angle to the pin won't be quite as good, but you'll still be in excellent shape.

Player C sets up as described with the driver and gives it his best shot. Impact feels solid, but he hits a pull that flies dead straight. He is waiting for the "banana ball," but the ball never curves off to the right. The ball flies 215 yards (the solidly hit pull usually goes a shade farther) and lands about 10 yards off the fairway, short of the woods but in thick Bermuda rough. Since hitting the ball left on a dogleg right lengthens the hole a little, Player C is looking at 135 to the middle of the green.

From a fairway lie, you'd probably be looking at a nice 6-iron from this distance. This shot is more complicated, though, and judging the lie is very important. Because the ball is sitting down slightly, in a depression, you must select a more lofted club.

Actually, if you carried a 9-wood in your bag, this would be a good place to use it, since it's easier to hit the ball up and out with. But you don't carry one, and your 5- or 7-wood is just too much club. Here's what I rec-ommend: Take a 7-iron. Play the ball in the middle of your stance with your

In playing a shot out of a slight depression in rough, make a three-quarter swing. This will prevent the wrists from overhinging on the backswing and casting on the downswing.

hands ahead. Keep the backswing compact, to prevent overhinging the wrists at the top and casting on the downswing. Here, because of the lie, you must pull the club down hard. At impact, the effective loft of your 7-iron will change to a 6-iron—the perfect club for the distance at hand.

Player C makes all these adjustments, puts a good compact swing on the ball, and the shot flies out low and straight to the front of the green. Great shot! You now face a long putt, but at least you hit the green.

Not a good first putt. You worried so much about direction control that you forgot about distance control.

Not a good second putt either. The reason you pushed the putt so badly was that you peeked. Bogey is not a bad score, and you avoided doing worse, but even for you this hole was a missed opportunity.

COMMON STRATEGIC AND SHOTMAKING ERRORS BY THE C PLAYER

- Not knowing how the ball's lie will affect the shot
- Making direction a priority over pace

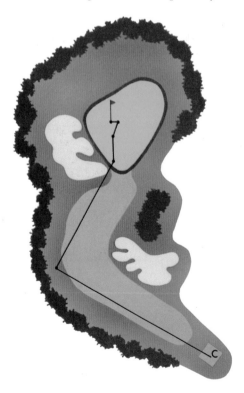

Butch's Lessons

The vast majority of high-handicappers do not adjust their planning of approach shots from the rough. They use the same club from a particular distance regardless of the lie. The only true secret to figuring out how to handle different lies, and being sure about club selection, is to experiment in practice. Empty a bucket of balls and simply determine how far you hit each club from various lies. As you create lies for yourself, let your imagination run wild. That way, nothing will surprise you out on the course.

The main reason you scored bogey, instead of par, was that bad first putt you hit short of the hole. The next time you're in this type of situation, try to see the putt rolling all the way to the hole—see it go in before you putt. This mental rehearsal will help you put the right amount of oomph behind the putt, and stop you from concentrating only on the putt's line. Distance is more important than line on long putts; if you hit it the right distance, you'll almost certainly be close enough for an easy second putt.

HOLE	1	2	3	4	5	6	7	8	9	OUT	
YARDS	366	380	485	177	368	373	103	515	356	3123	
PAR	4	4	5	3	4	4	3	5	4	36	
Player A	5	5	5	3	3	4	3	5	4	37	
Player B	5	6	5	4	5	5	4	5	4	43	
Player C	6	4	8	4	5	5	5	6	4	47	
HOLE	10	11	12	13	14	15	16	17	18	IN	TOTAL
YARDS	183	508	121	339	339	417	407	452	510	3276	6399
PAR	3	5	3	4	4	4	4	4	5	36	72
Player A	3	5	3	3							
Player B	3	5	3	4							
Player C	4	6	4	5							

Jack Nicklaus' Muirfield Village course, host of the PGA Tour's Memorial Tournament since 1976, will rank high on anyone's list of modern classics of American golf course architecture. This long and spacious course, built on rolling land a short distance northwest of Columbus, Ohio, received some criticism in early years as being "a course only Jack Nicklaus can play," because its length and heavily guarded greens favor the towering fade that was Nicklaus' trademark in his heyday. Gradually, this viewpoint has softened as the course has matured. Meanwhile, the list of winners at the Memorial has been full of Hall of Famers, adding to the course's reputation. Besides Nicklaus, Tom Watson, Greg Norman, and Hale Irwin are two-time winners, with Ray Floyd, Curtis Strange, and Tom Lehman also having entered the winner's circle.

Muirfield Village is known for its brutally long par 4s; however, we're going to test you on this great layout's shortest par 4. From the middle tees, it measures only 339 yards, the same number as the previous hole in our lineup. Yet it is one of the most testing short par 4s in golf. The hole is relatively straight and runs slightly downhill from the tee. You might think a really big knocker would want to pull out the driver and take a whack at the green, but the target is so tiny and so fiendishly guarded, to do so would be plain stupid.

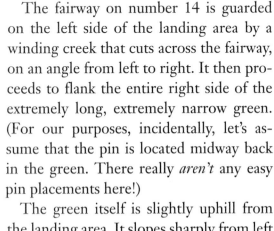

The fairway on number 14 is guarded on the left side of the landing area by a winding creek that cuts across the fairway, on an angle from left to right. It then proceeds to flank the entire right side of the extremely long, extremely narrow green. (For our purposes, incidentally, let's assume that the pin is located midway back in the green. There really *aren't* any easy pin placements here!)

The green itself is slightly uphill from the landing area. It slopes sharply from left to right, toward the creek, so that any pitch shot landing on the right side with backspin may suck back into the water. The green is lightning fast, so that putts from above the hole that roll into the water are also common. To make matters worse, two huge bunkers tightly guard the entire left side of the green, and they also slope downhill toward the creek. Thus, there is no room to bail out on your approach—a recovery shot from these bunkers is one terrifying shot.

In sum, if there is a more exacting short par 4 than the 14th at Muirfield Village, I'd like to see it. Let's consider how you should try to play it.

The A Player

For you, and the low-handicap player, this should not be a particularly hard tee shot. You don't need a lot of distance. However, you know darn well you want to hit your approach from the fairway. Trying to get on this green from the rough or trees is the best way to make a big number that I know of. So there's a little extra pressure to hit the tee shot on the short grass, and that in itself can make it tougher.

The ideal tee shot should be in the center of the fairway, 210 to 220 yards out. This will leave you safely short of the creek, with a nice full wedge or short iron in. Since the tee is a little elevated, as are most on this course, you'll get a little extra carry out of your shot. So your choice of club here should be a 2-iron or 3-iron.

This is another spot where you can't afford to get lazy just because you're hitting a lay-up off the tee. Imagine that you're playing a long par 3 and you're trying to knock it on the center of the green. Stay smooth and in rhythm, and release the clubhead.

Player A hit his tee shot, with a 3-iron, just a little thin, so that with the extra downhill carry, the ball is in the right-center of the fairway 210 yards out.

You've got about 130 yards left to the flag, which for you is probably a good solid 9-iron, particularly since the wind is not a real factor. The hilly and mostly treed Muirfield Village course is generally fairly well protected from severe winds.

From where you are, the long green runs at an angle from left to right and your line will be over the creek guarding the right-front of the green. The most obvious miss here is to bail out a little to the left, but there is so little margin for error here that even a slight bailout will put you in one of the bunkers. Believe it or not, putting it there might be as bad as hitting it into the water, because the sand shot is so difficult. So to be perfectly honest, you don't have much choice here. You have to go straight at the pin, or perhaps try to put the ball just left and short of it.

Player A lines up carefully, gets comfortable, and swings. Contact with his 9-iron is flush and as he looks up, the ball is flying high and heading straight for the stick. His excitement level leaps as he sees the ball land 15 feet short of the pin. Then he looks on in horror as the ball takes one soft hop, then spins back and starts to creep down, down to the right with the slope, finally tumbling into the creek! Player A is stunned.

By the standards of this hole you didn't quite hit two perfect shots. You actually hit that 9-iron a little too good, so that it came into the green with lots of backspin. With a green that slopes sharply to the right like this one, you actually need a softer shot, one that comes into the green more or less "dead," so that it stops pretty much where it lands. Don't hit down so abruptly. Just sort of nip the ball off the turf, by hitting the ball more on the through-swing.

When Player A gets to his ball, he notices that the ball is lying near the water's edge and is only half-submerged. And it's just 35 feet from the hole.

No! Don't take a drop! Whenever the ball is resting in water so that it is only half-submerged, this shot is playable because you can judge the ball's position accurately. (If it's completely underwater, you *should* take a penalty drop, because water refracts light and you may not be able to tell the ball's actual position. Also, when the ball's more than half-underwater, it is virtually impossible to dislodge it.)

In this case, however, you can definitely play the shot. First make sure you can take a reasonable stance, and that there are no objects such as rocks in the way of your downswing. Assuming you have a clear path, address the ball with your sand iron, making certain to hover the sole of the club a full inch or two above the water, with the clubface set slightly open. Touching the water would cost you a stroke penalty.

You're going to play this shot just like you would a partially buried ball in a bunker. That's why you want the face open. You also want the leading edge of your wedge to cut through the water and get under the ball. If you lay the face way open, the leading edge might skull the ball so that you drill it into the bank right in front of you.

When the ball is only half-submerged in water by the green, that's a "green light" situation. Play a sand iron and blast the ball out.

But really, this is not that difficult a shot. Play the shot just as you would a bunker shot, with the ball just ahead of center in your stance. Keep your weight favoring your left side and swing the club up with your arms, keeping your head very still. Then pull the club down into the water on a steep angle, aiming for a spot about two inches behind the ball. Because you have water rather than sand resisting your clubhead, swing with just a little more force than you would for a sand shot of the same distance.

You'll probably be holding your breath as you play this one, but if you follow my directions, you'll be amazed at the result.

The ball popped up and out beautifully. In fact, it came out a little too well, finishing 15 feet beyond the hole. Now Player A is left with a very quick downhiller that most first-timers will hit way past the hole. He can't really try to make this. He should just try to find the right line and then just get the ball in motion.

All right, he doesn't can it, but he leaves it within 18 inches of the hole. He taps in, and gets out of Dodge with a wet bogey 5.

Count your blessings.

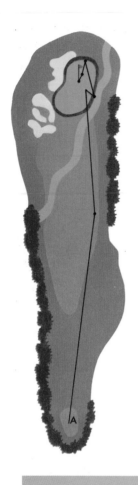

- Not releasing fully on the tee shot
- Hitting short-iron approaches with too much spin when you don't need it

Butch's Lessons

Often, when the better player is just trying to hit the fairway off the tee on a tough hole like this one, he or she will tend to steer the clubhead through impact rather than trust the normal free release. If the hands do not uncock fully at impact, the tendency will be for the club to come in a little high on the ball and/or a touch open in relation to the target. This means a thin shot that usually misses to the right. Remember, once you've picked your target on a tight-driving hole, make the best swing you can, and that always includes a free release of the clubhead through impact.

DRILL (FOR ENHANCING THE RELEASE OF THE HANDS, ARMS, AND CLUB)

Take your address with a 5-iron, then drop your right hand down so that your hands are a few inches apart. Swing. Immediately, you should feel the correct sensation of your right hand and forearm crossing over your left hand and forearm through impact. Now, grip your driver normally and incorporate this releasing action into your swing. The result: more solid shots hit off the sweet spot of the clubface.

There are times when you *don't* want to put too much backspin on a full short-iron or wedge shot. With the banked green at number 14 (or one like it at your home course), severe backspin can take the ball all the way off the green and into the creek. In cases like this, you don't want to hit the shot hard. Take one more club than normal, grip down the shaft one-half inch, then make a very smooth swing with no noticeable acceleration through impact. You'll get a soft-flying shot that comes to a stop a few feet from where it lands rather than jerking back—in this case into a hazard.

The B Player

You also want to hit the ball to the center of the fairway about 210 to 220 yards off this tee. While the A player went with a long iron off this tee, I think you're smart to go with a 3-wood. The reasoning is that you don't want to lay up too far back, because you know you'll face a very tough shot into this green.

Player B sets up carefully to the ball, focuses in on a small target area in the middle of the fairway, and swings. However, the ball starts down the left side of the fairway and hooks left, into the creek.

Bad shots are a part of the game, and the better you become at shrugging them off, the better golfer you'll be. Look at it this way: If you hit every shot exactly the way you wanted, you wouldn't be carrying a handicap between 10 and 16. (To avoid this type of shot in the future, be sure to shift your weight onto your left foot at the start of the downswing. Also, striving for a high finish will discourage "flipping" the club into a closed position at impact.)

One way to cure a hook is to be sure to swing into a high finish position.

Player B takes a penalty drop, within two clublengths of where the ball entered the hazard. His lie is average, and the ball is 140 yards from the pin, or within 7-iron distance. If he has any advantage here, it's that from this angle he'll be shooting along the length of the green rather than somewhat across it. If he can land the ball on the front edge of the green, it will release toward the hole.

He makes his swing, and contact is good, but he's pulled the shot just the slightest amount. Still, the flight of the ball is off enough for the shot to land in the first big bunker to the left of the green. He now faces a shot not even the pros want—a downhill, sidehill sand shot with water beyond the pin. And he lies 3.

Well, Butch, you might be saying, what do I do now? In order to get the ball close, you'd have to hit a high, soft bunker shot that lands pin-high on the left fringe, close to the second bunker, and let it trickle down to the hole. In other words, a world-class shot. My advice: Don't try it. Instead, your goal should be to pop the ball out over the lip, and let the ball roll so that it finishes short and right of the hole. Forget the hole and just play a basic short sand shot into the fat of the green. Open the blade, pick a spot two to three inches behind the ball, keep your head steady, and just pop the ball out with a short swing.

Player B executes well here. The ball lands a foot or two onto the green, in line with the hole, but then dribbles away to the right, stopping 25 feet below the hole. He has an easier putt now, uphill although still breaking to the right. He makes a good stroke, but the ball breaks more than he thinks and stops two feet below the cup. He lines up the straight-in second putt and holes it for a double-bogey 6.

You're shaking your head and wondering how you could goof up such a short hole. But let me encourage you by pointing out that you managed your mistakes pretty well here. If your strategy hadn't been sound, you could easily have scored 8.

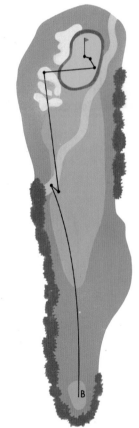

COMMON STRATEGIC AND SHOTMAKING ERRORS BY THE B PLAYER
- Hitting hooks from the tee
- Slight pull shots into the green

Butch's Lessons

You shouldn't panic about the hook you hit off the tee. Your grip just got a little too strong, meaning that the Vs formed by the thumbs and forefingers of your hands pointed up at your right shoulder. I'm all for a "strongish" hold that sees the Vs pointing midway between the chin and right shoulder, simply because this grip promotes a better forearm rotation on the backswing and a more fluid release of the club on the downswing.

Another thing that will discourage a left arm chicken-wing position and a dominant right hand—and cure a hook—is to concentrate on finishing lower and more around your body. Incidentally, swinging into a full finish will also help you stop pulling iron shots.

The C Player

Player C wisely selects a 3-wood, but fails to release the club again, and slices the ball 15 yards off the fairway into the right rough. He's now 160 yards from the middle of the green, and up ahead, a stand of trees blocks his direct line to the hole. He's got to lay up short of the water.

Frankly, it's just as well that you're blocked out from the green. For a high-handicapper to try for the perfect shot, out of rough, over the creek but short of the bunkers behind this narrow green, would be very dumb golf. Instead, you want to punch the ball back out to the middle of the fairway, safely short of the creek, then try to pitch on and two-putt for your bogey.

At this point, don't make the error I see high-handicappers commit so often, which is to play a slaphappy punch out of the rough. What happens a lot is they hit the shot too hard, so the ball runs across into the rough on the opposite side or, as here, into the creek crossing the fairway. You've probably got about 75 yards to the creek at the middle of the fairway. Take a 9-iron or pitching wedge and play a pitch-and-run shot of no more than 60 yards.

Good. You're now in the middle of the fairway, with about 110 yards to the hole, slightly uphill. This should be a 9-iron for you or possibly a smooth 8. Whichever you choose, commit to the club and to making a compact, controlled but aggressive swing with it. Too many amateurs get too worried about hitting a "hard 9" or a "soft 8" to the point where they don't even make a good swing. Commit to the club and then focus on your target and on simply making a good swing, and you'll come out way ahead.

Player C goes with the 9-iron. He makes solid contact and the ball flies nicely on line, landing on the front edge of the green and trickling to a stop 35 feet from the hole. He still has a shot at par, albeit a fairly long shot.

Player C, thinking he has little chance to sink the putt, rushes his routine and ends up leaving the ball on the low side, three feet from the hole. To his credit, he takes his time on the next putt, holing out for a bogey 5.

COMMON STRATEGIC AND SHOTMAKING ERRORS BY THE C PLAYER

- Hitting "lay-up" shots into more trouble
- Rushing long putts that you don't expect to make

Butch's Lessons

In this case, Player C played a fine lay-up shot. However, just in case you have trouble in this department, here's some advice that should help.

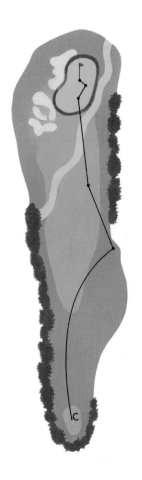

Obviously, the higher your handicap, the more likely you are to hit shots into trouble. When you do, you can't afford to compound the error with a sloppily played recovery shot. From rough or woods, check carefully for any branches you need to keep the ball under, and select a club that will help you accomplish that. Gauge how far it is to get the ball to the fairway and how far it is to the rough or hazards you want to keep the ball short of. Decide on the total distance you need to hit the shot, and take a practice swing or two to get the feel for a swing that will produce that distance. Play the ball in the middle of your stance, make a short half-swing, and bring your arms and club through while keeping your hands and wrists "dead" to keep from scooping at the ball and hitting it fat.

The sooner you learn to give all length putts your fullest attention, the better you'll score. Just because you face a 25-footer on a fast green, one you think you have little chance of holing, doesn't mean you should just set up quickly and hit the ball. Pick the line, set your putter down precisely on it, use your normal prestroke routine, and make a decisive stroke.

HOLE	1	2	3	4	5	6	7	8	9	OUT	
YARDS	366	380	485	177	368	373	103	515	356	3123	
PAR	4	4	5	3	4	4	3	5	4	36	
Player A	5	5	5	3	3	4	3	5	4	37	
Player B	5	6	5	4	5	5	4	5	4	43	
Player C	6	4	8	4	5	5	5	6	4	47	

HOLE	10	11	12	13	14	15	16	17	18	IN	TOTAL
YARDS	183	508	121	339	339	417	407	452	510	3276	6399
PAR	3	5	3	4	4	4	4	4	5	36	72
Player A	3	5	3	3	5						
Player B	3	5	3	4	6						
Player C	4	6	4	5	5						

THE COUNTRY CLUB OF BROOKLINE
Par 4: 417 yards

The Country Club of Brookline, located in Brookline, Massachusetts, is a pure golf club that was organized in 1882. The course itself, a traditional design, puts a premium on accuracy, both from the tee and on approach shots. Narrow rolling fairways are bordered by thick rough plus tall oaks and maples. The fast greens are so tiny that golfers playing the course for the first time as guests often comment that they look like pancakes. That's not to suggest that they are flat, however; many of the greens at Brookline are undulating, so in order to put yourself in position to charge a birdie putt or to two-putt from long distance, you'd better keep the ball below the cup. In most cases, the tiny greens are also surrounded by deep bunkers that require players to hit soft-landing recovery shots in order to save par.

Brookline, long recognized as one of the premier golf courses in America, first gained popularity in 1913, when 20-year-old amateur and local boy Francis Ouimet beat Great Britain's two greatest champions, Harry Vardon and Ted Ray, in an 18-hole playoff to win the United States Open Championship. Ray, the long hitter of

the trio, was expected to win, because he had the ability to play more-lofted clubs into the greens and, too, possessed the strength to recover well from the heavy rough. Ironically, Ray was the first to drop out of contention after bogeying the 15th hole, the same one you will be playing today.

Since that famous Open, Brookline has hosted the Open twice: in 1963, when smooth-swinging Julius Boros defeated Arnold Palmer and Jacky Cupit in a playoff, and in 1988, when Curtis Strange beat Nick Faldo, also in an 18-hole playoff. One big reason why Boros and Strange scored so well during the championships and in the playoffs was that they scored well on hole 15.

The 15th is a par 4 of 417 yards. It plays shorter than it looks, however, because you hit from an elevated tee. Although a roadway runs across the fairway, the biggest trouble off the tee is the rough that borders the fairway. If the ball sits down in the grass, which it does more often than not, you will be forced to lay up with a medium or short iron. When laying up, you must be careful not to land in a lone fairway bunker. The green itself is well guarded by three traps—one on the left, one behind, one on the right side. Let's see how you do.

Player A

In order to set yourself in position to attack the flag you must hit a very solid tee shot, preferably down the right center of the fairway. Although a draw is your natural shot, you may want to consider hitting a power fade off the tee, since that will make it easier for you to land the ball in the ideal spot.

Player A said he felt more comfortable starting the ball down the right edge of the fairway and having it draw back to the center. I had no problem with that decision, since it's important to be mentally sure of the shot you intend to play. When doubt creeps in, you usually run into trouble.

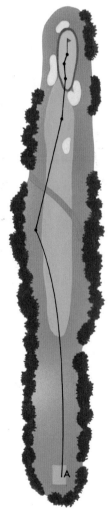

Player A seems to make a good golf swing, but starts the ball well right of where he wants, and actually hits more of a hook than a draw. The ball lands 240 yards out from the tee, but in thick rough to the left. From there, he plays an intelligent shot with a 9-iron, advancing the ball down the fairway, to within 50 yards of the green.

I don't like the third shot he plays. In trying to hit a delicate soft pitch all the way to the pin with a sand wedge, he leaves the ball on the green but well short. He two-putts for bogey.

COMMON STRATEGIC AND SHOTMAKING ERRORS BY THE A PLAYER

- Using a driver with a medium-flex shaft
- Playing the wrong type of pitch from near the green

Butch's Lessons

Having watched you now for 15 holes, I know that you are more of a hitter than a swinger. Let's face it, you like to swing hard. That doesn't bother me. I'll just give you the same advice I give Tiger: *I don't care how fast you swing as long as you stay balanced.* What does bother me is the shaft in your driver. No, not that it's steel instead of graphite or titanium, but that it is medium-flex. You have obviously become stronger since the day you bought this club. For that reason, you have outgrown it. Go to your local pro and have him change the shaft to a stiff-flex, and the clubhead will stay behind your hands longer, so you can hit later. Now, the clubhead is actually being whipped into the ball too quickly—before you shift your weight to your left foot and clear your hips. The clubhead is leading your hands and the clubface is closing too dramatically. Under pressure, you tend to hit a hook. You won't hit such an uncontrollable shot once you change the shaft in your driver.

Generally, strong players who sometimes duck-hook the ball should not use a driver with a flexible shaft.

The third shot you played was not the percentage play. Whenever the green is unguarded in the front, and the fairway grass is mowed low, hit a running pitch shot that lands short of the green, or on its front portion, then rolls to the hole. You can still play your sand wedge; just move the ball back in your stance, make a short backswing, and let the hands lead the club through impact.

The B Player

This hole sets up well for your fade. Ideally, you'll want to start it down the center of the fairway, then let it drift slightly right. If you catch it solidly, you'll face a fairly straightforward second shot that I know you can handle easily.

The good news: Player B faithfully goes through his preswing routine, aims correctly, makes a beautiful swing, and hits the ball 220 yards down the fairway. The bad news: His ball lands in a divot.

He correctly sets up with the ball back in his stance, and keeps his hands ahead through impact, but the ball flies too far, landing over the green. He swings a little hard, I think, because he thought he had to dig the ball out of the divot, and because he was a little mad about his bad break.

He concentrates hard on his chip, playing a good shot. A solid putt helps him score a well-earned par.

COMMON STRATEGIC AND SHOTMAKING ERRORS BY THE B PLAYER

- Not mentally accepting a bad break
- Hitting the wrong club from a divot

Butch's Lessons

Golf is a game of good and bad breaks, and during a round of 18 holes they usually even out. No one likes to hit a good drive and find the ball lying in a divot. But it's something that you will have to deal with from time to time.

In handling this shot, your first mistake was choosing the wrong club. You chose your 5-wood, which is a club you normally hit from 200 yards out. To recover from this lie, you must swing the club back on a steeper angle and hit down more sharply. You must know that because you swung correctly and led the club nicely into the ball with the hands. What you don't realize is that a steep angle of attack actually reduces the effective loft of the club; the 5-wood you hit was actually like a 4-wood. That's why you went over the green. Next time, hit your 7-wood, and swing only a trifle harder than normal. Don't go after the ball like you did. The ball will fly like a 5-wood and finish on the green.

The C Player

This is a tough hole, so play it as a par-5. Remember, that's your personal par on a difficult par-4 hole such as this. Scoring par is like scoring birdie.

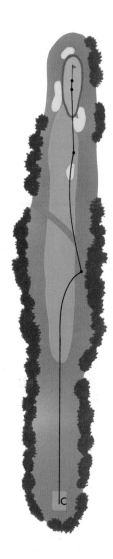

The proper strategy for you is to play for your slice off the tee, lay up short of the green, pitch up to around 25 feet, and two-putt for 5.

Player C has trouble getting aimed properly. He keeps jockeying his feet and body into position. The fact that the wind is blowing left to right slightly may be making him more nervous about hitting his slice into deep trouble. Eventually, he does pull the trigger, but slices the ball 210 yards into the light rough bordering the right side of the fairway.

The grass is growing toward the target, and had he known how to play this shot he could have reached the green with his second shot. He hits down on the ball much too hard, and on too steep an angle. As a result, he hits the ball fat. In fact, he is lucky to carry the fairway bunker down by the green.

From that point he plays an excellent pitch-and-run shot, then saves par with a good solid putt.

COMMON STRATEGIC AND SHOTMAKING ERRORS BY THE C PLAYER

- Not visualizing the shot
- Not using the right technique in light rough

Butch's Lessons

I could tell from the length of time you took to play your drive that this tee shot intimidated you. I noticed that you shuffled your feet around and kept regripping the club. If you find yourself doing that, you're expressing doubt to yourself about the shot you're preparing to hit. Don't be afraid to back away from the shot, and reset yourself from the start of your preshot routine.

I also noticed that, while you were getting set, you never looked down the fairway. Watch the pros. They look at the ball, then up at their target area in the fairway a few times before swinging. It's important to "see" your ball land in a specific area of the fairway before you even hit it. This healthy mental preparation helps prevent you from steering the swing, and slicing.

When you got in the rough, you swung the club on too steep a plane for the lie you had. Any time the ball is sitting relatively cleanly in light rough, and you want to get more distance out of the shot, swing on a flatter plane than normal. This will encourage blades of grass to fill the grooves of the club at impact, so that you purposely hit a flyer and hit the ball farther. Had you used this technique, you would have probably putted for birdie. Still, nice par.

When the ball is in light rough, and you seek more distance, hit a "flyer." Do that by swinging on a flatter plane and sweeping through the ball in the impact zone.

HOLE	1	2	3	4	5	6	7	8	9	OUT	
YARDS	366	380	485	177	368	373	103	515	356	3123	
PAR	4	4	5	3	4	4	3	5	4	36	
Player A	5	5	5	3	3	4	3	5	4	37	
Player B	5	6	5	4	5	5	4	5	4	43	
Player C	6	4	8	4	5	5	5	6	4	47	

HOLE	10	11	12	13	14	15	16	17	18	IN	TOTAL
YARDS	183	508	121	339	339	417	407	452	510	3276	6399
PAR	3	5	3	4	4	4	4	4	5	36	72
Player A	3	5	3	3	5	5					
Player B	3	5	3	4	6	4					
Player C	4	6	4	5	5	4					

MERION GOLF CLUB
Par 4: 407 yards

Located along Philadelphia's Main Line in an elite suburban area, Merion is the site of some of golf's most historic moments. Merion is the course where a 14-year-old Bobby Jones competed in his first national tournament; where, in 1924, he won the first of his five U.S. Amateur titles; and where he completed his epic 1930 Grand Slam with another victory in the U.S. Amateur. The U.S. Open has been held four times here, with Ben Hogan's playoff win in 1950, only a little more than a year after his near-fatal auto crash, being one of golf's most famous events.

Merion has not been as much in the limelight since the last U.S. Open was held there in 1981 (won by David Graham). At a total length of 6544 yards and a par of 70, the course is considered a little too short for modern major championship play, and it is also difficult to shoehorn large galleries into its tight confines. Still, Merion is a wonderful test of golf. The back nine has a par of 34 and is only 3120 yards in length from the back tees, and holes 10 through 15 in particular offer some good birdie opportunities for the better player. However, the 16th hole, which you will be playing, begins a long and intimidating final stretch, the "quarry" holes; comprising two par 4s sandwiching a long par 3, all three holes require you to traverse a rugged quarry on one of the full shots.

The 16th, 430 yards from the championship tee, plays at 407 yards for the members. The hole is very curiously shaped. From the tee, it appears that it's a fairly straight hole, working downhill off the tee with a long uphill second shot over the quarry to the green. Actually, the design of the hole allows for it to be safely played in three full shots: The fairway winds around to the right of the quarry, then curls back to the left as it nears the green. However, most golfers, if they hit a decent drive, will want to shoot directly at the green on their second shots, or will otherwise lay up short of the quarry and pitch over it with their third.

The 16th is not a particularly difficult driving hole. There are fairway bunkers on either side, but the fairway is relatively wide. Also, most good drives from the regular men's tees will finish well beyond the bunkers. The fairway slopes from right to left in the landing area, and the best location for the drive to land is the left side of the fairway. From here, you'll have a flatter lie and also a better view of, and angle to, the green.

The two-tiered putting surface sits up above the rough ground, brushland, and bunkers within the quarry. You have about 10 to 12 yards of mowed rough between the edge of the quarry and the front of the green, so even though the shot is intimidating, it is possible to get away with a slight "miss" and avoid a lost ball or an un-playable lie.

There are two bunkers well to the right of the green, but they don't come into play often. A greater concern, especially with the pin on the back tier as we will assume it is here, is that there's a drop-off immediately behind the green. Should you "air-mail" the green, a bogey or worse is almost guaranteed.

No matter how you get it, a par on Merion's 16th should be ap-preciated, a birdie cherished.

The A Player

There's not much of a decision to be made off this tee. You should hit the driver. You can carry the ball beyond the bunkers with it, and this is one hole where you want to have as short an iron into the green as possible.

Although the fairway is generous, don't be lax on the tee shot. Pick a small spot near the center of the fairway and focus your con-centration on it. Your ideal shot here will be a draw which, along with the slight right-to-left slope of the fairway, would bring your ball to rest on the left side. As always, keep your swing smooth and deliberate.

Player A nails the drive, starting it just right of center, but it draws a little and takes some extra roll with the sideslope, so that it winds up in the left-center of the fairway and 265 yards out. He couldn't have walked it out there any better.

You have just 142 yards to the middle of the green, but with the pin on the back tier, you have about 150 to the hole, and the shot will play 5 yards longer since it's a little uphill. That's a good 7-iron for you (the wind is not a factor). This shot presents an interesting question: Do you fly the ball to the back half of the green, or do you play a lower punch shot, possibly with a 6-iron, and hope it runs up the slope? This could be argued either way. The punch is probably the safer shot, but there is enough room on the back half of the green to hit the green and hold it. And you've been swinging well.

Player A decides to hit the full 7-iron. He sets up aiming just to the left of the flag but with the clubface square to it, hoping to put a touch of fade on the shot to help it stop quickly. His timing is just a shade fast, however. He hits the shot left of the pin and there's no cut-spin on the ball.

The next time you want to hit a fade, weaken your grip slightly by moving your hands toward the target slightly.

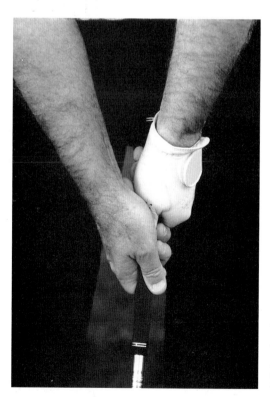

A weak grip will help you hit a controlled fade.

The ball lands on the back tier and hops over the green by about 8 feet, into some sticky rough but short of the downslope. Player A faces a downhill, sidehill chip back to the hole, which is 40 feet away.

Not great, given the position you were in off the tee. You'll have to lob the ball over about 15 feet of rough and fringe on your line to the hole, then let it trickle the rest of the way to the cup. Align your sand or lob wedge toward the spot where you want the ball to land, 4 to 5 feet to the left of a direct line to the hole. Your stance should be narrow and open. Make a slow, wristy backswing so that the clubhead moves up quickly and returns fairly steeply down onto the ball. Keep your head still until well beyond impact.

Player A's shot pops up nicely, but it lands to the right and a little short of his interim target. It kicks right with the slope and rolls slowly to a stop about 10 feet short of the cup. Not a terrible shot, but not his best either from this position. Now he has to sweat to score par.

Player A leaves the par putt short, on the low side, and must settle for bogey.

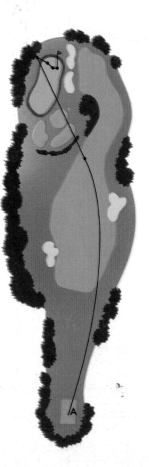

COMMON STRATEGIC AND SHOTMAKING ERRORS BY THE A PLAYER

- "Fighting" the design of the hole
- Leaving 10-foot putts short

Butch's Lessons

Many good golfers don't score as well as they could because they don't play the type of shot a certain hole asks for. The smarter play on the approach would have been the lower-flying iron that landed on the front half of the green. Even if it doesn't release and stays on the lower level, you're still better off than you are in the rough over the green. The odds are that you will two-putt more often from 50 feet below the hole, than you will get it up and down from the rough behind the green chipping downhill. (Like I said, though, if it's your desire to hit a full shot with cut-spin, weaken your grip.)

When you came up short this time on your putt, I noticed that you cut across the ball. This slows the speed of the ball and sends it rolling off line. Hitting through the putt, with the club moving straight along the target line at impact, is a technical must. To encourage this type of path, keep your arms and hands closer to your body and the putterhead moving low to the ground.

DRILL (FOR ENCOURAGING A STRAIGHT-BACK, STRAIGHT-THROUGH SHORT-PUTT STROKE)

Plant two parallel rows of six tees in the green, the rows about three inches apart. The width of the path between them should be only slightly wider than the width of your putter. Practice swinging the putter back and through without hitting the tees. In no time, you'll get rid of your out-to-in cut stroke.

The B Player

The 10-to-16-handicap player who is capable of hitting a well-struck drive 230 yards under normal conditions should try to do just that here. You'd like to get as far down the fairway as possible to allow a player with your average length to have a medium-length iron to the green.

Ideally, you'd like to hit a slight draw, because such a shot would give you extra roll rather than working into the slideslope in the fairway, forcing the ball to a halt quickly when it lands. To help you put some draw-spin on the ball (as well as gain maximum distance), remember to tee it a touch higher than you would normally. Stay loose prior to the takeaway and swing freely.

Like Player A, Player B makes pure contact. The ball flies high and almost dead straight, but it doesn't draw, so it lands in the left-center of the fairway, 240 yards out. He's left with approximately 175 yards to the pin, hitting slightly uphill, so the shot will actually play about 180.

This is the distance you will normally get with a well-struck 3-iron. Keep in mind, though, that you'd rather not repeat the fate of Player A and hit a hot-landing shot that ends up over the green—an easy thing to do with even a well-struck long-iron shot. You'd like to come into this green with a shot that is fairly high. This would assure that if you carried the ball to the middle of the green, it would either stay just below the upslope in the green or maybe crawl over it so you'd finish close to the pin—but you would not run over.

Of course, the high long iron is not easy for amateurs like you to execute. For one thing, you instinctively try to hit the ball harder with long irons than with any other clubs. This creates a lot of unnecessary head movement, which in itself causes a higher percentage of mishits than with other clubs. Also, most of this excessive head movement is toward the target on the downswing, so that even if you make good contact, the clubface is delofted so that the result is a "worm burner."

Here's what you need to do: Take your 3-iron and set up to the ball just a trifle open, aligned about 20 feet left of the flag. Position the ball about one ball-width farther forward than normal, directly opposite your left heel.

You need to make a smooth, level swing here to apply the 22 or 23 degrees of loft on the face of your 3-iron squarely through the ball. Concentrate on keeping your head very still and behind the ball at impact. This will allow you to clip the ball neatly off the turf rather than digging too deep. Strive for a full, high follow-through.

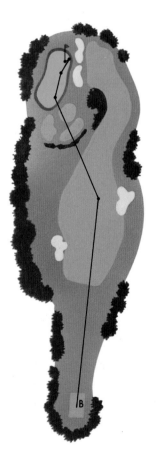

Player B hits the ball fairly solidly but it fades a little, costing him vital yardage. The ball lands on the right-front of the green, climbs the slope slightly, then drifts back down to the front-right corner of the green, 50 feet from the hole. Not exactly what he wants—but then if he hit the green with every 3-iron he ever hit, he'd be playing on tour.

Player B faces a difficult putt that moves sharply uphill for the middle third of the putt's length and also breaks to the left as it works its way over the crown. He takes a few practice strokes and decides on a line starting about two feet to the right of the hole. He makes the stroke, and almost automatically after impact he whispers, "Get up!" His senses prove correct—he didn't give the putt enough "juice." It has enough speed to clear the crown, but just barely, as it comes to rest 13 feet short of the hole.

Player B lines up his second putt carefully, and keeps his head still as he makes his stroke. However, he pushes the ball slightly, missing it on the right. He taps the ball in for a disappointing bogey.

COMMON STRATEGIC AND SHOTMAKING EFFORTS
BY THE B PLAYER
- Swinging noticeably harder than normal with the long irons
- Failing to judge the force needed on uphill, two-tiered putts

Butch's Lessons

While it's true that long irons are harder to hit well than short irons or lofted fairway woods, you're only making matters worse if you try to "muscle" them. What you need to do when playing long irons is to make square and precise impact on the club's sweet spot. It's definitely harder to do this if you're trying to hit the shot extra-hard, no matter what club you're using. So, whenever you have a long iron to the green, try imagining you're hitting a 9-iron instead. Just make your normal 9-iron swing with the long iron. You'll be amazed at how much better shots you'll hit.

Many amateurs misjudge how hard to hit putts whenever they're putting up to a cup on an upper tier. Get in the habit of reading these putts carefully from a side angle, well away from the line of the putt. This will give you a much better perspective on how much force you'll really need in the stroke.

The C Player

The 16th at Merion is truly a challenging hole for you. Your average-length drive, in the fairway, will give you a chance to get home in two, but you'll likely need two woods, with the second traversing the ravine. The play from the tee, though, is to hit the driver, because using a shorter stick just about guarantees you'll have to lay up.

Your line on this hole should be down the left edge of the fairway, since your tee shots almost always move left to right, sometimes quite drastically, in fact. Remember to tee the ball higher than normal, to give yourself a better chance of hitting the driver straight. Keep the swing tempo smooth and try to swing the clubhead level through the ball.

Player C chops down on the ball and hits what is more or less his standard tee shot—a high, soft fade that starts down the left-center and lands softly on the right-center of the fairway. The reason: He reverse-pivoted on the backswing, then dropped his right shoulder dramatically at the start of the downswing. The ball comes to rest only 195 yards down the fairway. With the ball on the right side of the fairway, he faces a tough hanging lie, with the ball above his feet. That back-right pin is very inaccessible—and 215 yards away.

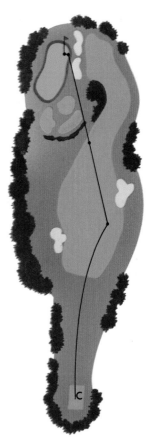

It's obvious that you should lay up instead of going for the green. But you must lay up correctly. You've got about 125 yards to the edge of the quarry, downhill, but only 115 yards to the edge of the fairway on your side of it. You'll want to play your third from the fairway, of course, so the correct lay-up should be about 100 to 110 yards, to the left side of the fairway.

Player C hits a less than perfect shot, but it works out perfectly, running down to a spot 10 yards from the end of the fairway. He's got 110 yards uphill to the hole. That might be a hard 9-iron for him, but he decides, wisely, to play a three-quarter shot with an 8-iron. His intent is to land the ball on the lower tier and let the ball run up, maybe even close to the flag.

Good thinking. Be sure to play the ball in

the middle of your stance (or slightly behind the centerpoint), choke down on the grip an inch for control, and make a compact, firm swing.

Player C's punch shot looks good. It flies on a line just right of the flag, lands on the lower level, and skips up onto the top tier, finishing just past pin-high and a mere 12 feet from the hole.

This is one of the better shots you've played today. It's a good lesson both in course management and in never giving up. Your putt breaks a little right-to-left, and is a little downhill. You can't gun this one. Instead, play an inch extra break and try to roll the ball at a speed that will just trickle it past the hole if it doesn't drop.

Player C follows my instructions. The ball takes the break just enough to drop softly into the cup. What a par! On one of the more intimidating par 4s on the course.

COMMON STRATEGIC AND SHOTMAKING ERRORS BY THE C PLAYER

- Employing a reverse-pivot action on the backswing, and not swinging levelly with the driver
- Failing to make the proper setup adjustments when playing from uneven lies

Butch's Lessons

Most higher-handicap players chop down on the ball with their long clubs, costing them a lot of distance. You'll transmit the greatest amount of energy to the ball if the face of your driver meets the back of the ball while it is traveling parallel to the ground. To give yourself a better chance of sweeping the ball off the tee with a level blow, turn your left knee inward on the backswing. This will allow you to shift your weight correctly on the backswing, then onto your left foot coming down. You'll also enhance the turning actions of your shoulders, and stop the right one from dropping down dramatically.

I see so many average to poorer golfers who don't take into account the terrain they'll be hitting from when they set up for shots from the fairway. Whenever the ball is above or below your feet, uphill or downhill, you should always take a good look at the shot from behind the ball. As a general rule, you want to position the ball closer to the *higher* foot—i.e., off a downhill lie, play the ball nearer your back foot; off an uphill lie, play it closer to your front heel. Also, you should always tilt your body so you're perpendicular to the slope—in effect you're giving yourself a flat lie. And be sure to swing within yourself; it's easy to lose your balance and mishit the ball if you swing too hard.

Turning your left knee behind the ball will enhance your weight-shift action on the backswing. As a result, you will make a solid weight shift on the downswing, and not drop your right shoulder dramatically.

When the ball's above your feet, aim right to allow for the draw flight that results from this lie; below your feet, aim left to allow for the fade.

Understanding these adjustments will make a big difference in how many greens you hit, turning a lot of bogeys and doubles into pars.

HOLE	1	2	3	4	5	6	7	8	9	OUT	
YARDS	366	380	485	177	368	373	103	515	356	3123	
PAR	4	4	5	3	4	4	3	5	4	36	
Player A	5	5	5	3	3	4	3	5	4	37	
Player B	5	6	5	4	5	5	4	5	4	43	
Player C	6	4	8	4	5	5	5	6	4	47	

HOLE	10	11	12	13	14	15	16	17	18	IN	TOTAL
YARDS	183	508	121	339	339	417	407	452	510	3276	6399
PAR	3	5	3	4	4	4	4	4	5	36	72
Player A	3	5	3	3	5	5	5				
Player B	3	5	3	4	6	4	5				
Player C	4	6	4	5	5	4	4				

OAK HILL COUNTRY CLUB
Par 4: 452 yards

For the 17th hole, I have a bit of a change of pace in store for you. The 17th, chosen from Rochester, New York's Oak Hill C.C., where my brother Craig Harmon is the head professional, is unusual in that the "members' tees" are set farther back than the tournament tees! You see, for members the hole is 458 yards, but it's played as a par 5. From the tournament tees, it is 452 yards but a par 4. This is how the hole played during the 1995 Ryder Cup matches, in which the European team defeated the U.S. by the narrowest of margins.

The 17th is part of a punishing finish of three straight par 4s of at least 440 yards. It might be fun to give you a taste of what it's like to play the hole from the Ryder Cup tees. True, the difference between the two sets of markers is only 6 yards. But on the psychological side, the difference between playing a hole as a par 4 and as a par 5 can be remarkable. If it's played as a par 5, the amateur usually feels as though there's a little leeway and you can get home easily with three decent shots. But played as a par 4, the pressure is on, and that can make all the difference.

According to Craig, when played as a par 4, the 17th at Oak Hill is the toughest hole on the course. The hole is uphill off the tee with the top of the hill about a 230-yard carry away. The fairway then doglegs to the right in the landing area, and is tree-lined on both sides. If you drive long enough to carry the crest of the hill, the fairway begins to work downhill, but it also slopes to the left, so that a long, straight drive can easily run through the fairway and into the left woods.

All this means that, ideally, you need to carry your driver at least 230 yards uphill, so you'll get some downhill roll on the ball, and the shot must be faded (but not too much) to keep it on the fairway and out of the woods on either side. Pretty simple, huh? And if you manage to accomplish this, your reward will be a long shot to the green from a hanging lie that is both downhill and sidehill to the left. For those who can't reach the green in two, there are a pair of fairway bunkers lurking perhaps 75 yards short of the green. Then, as is shown clearly in this chapter's opening photograph, two more long, punishing bunkers narrow the entrance to the green itself, and there's another directly in back of the green for those who overhit slightly. In sum, the second shot is probably no easier than the first.

The green itself is large. However, it has three distinct sections. The front section, which, unusually, is a higher level, is possibly the hardest section to play to. Although it shortens the hole when the pin is here, this is the narrowest part of the green, and it's menaced by those two big bunkers. If you do hit the target, it's tough to keep the ball on the front section. The middle level of the green is probably the easiest to play to, as it's the lowest level and shots tend to funnel there. The back tier (where we'll say the pin is for your play on this hole) is the second-hardest section to play to. The hole obviously plays longer, and you must hit the shot with enough force to get over the upslope just past the center of the green, but not so hard as to reach the back bunker. The plus when the pin is back is that you have a wider target to shoot to than you do at the front.

As you read about these difficulties, I couldn't say I'd blame you if you're muttering to yourself, "What are you doing to me, Butch?" All I can say is, the 17th at Oak Hill is definitely one heck of a hole. Let me see if I can guide you to a par 4 here.

The A Player

Frankly, if you want to make a 4 on this hole, there's not a lot of strategy to consider from the tee. You have to go with the driver. Your average well-hit drive travels about 250 yards, and you need to carry it 230 to get to the top of the hill. Anything less than a solid drive will not get over the top, making it difficult if not impossible to get home in two.

Player A goes with the driver, planning to hit it down the left-center with a fade. And he hits it right on the screws, but the ball flies dead straight instead of fading. When he gets out to the landing area, he finds that the ball has rolled through the fairway, into medium-deep rough. The ball is not lying too badly. He has a clear shot to the green, but, with the pin on the green's back tier, he's all of 210 yards away.

You must have noted by now that I have been preaching intelligent, conservative strategy, and you probably are expecting me to tell you to lay up short of the green from here. In this case, not so. There are a few things working to your advantage here. First, you didn't go so far through the fairway that you're blocked out from the green, and second, your lie is not bad. You're at a distance where a good 5-wood will get you home. Last, the pin on the back level is an advantage because you're hitting from the rough; if you get the ball to the green it will release upon landing, perhaps helping you get to the back level.

This might be a good point at which to add that I think all amateurs will benefit from carrying a lofted metalwood such as a 5-wood. It will really help on long par 4s and par 5s in playing from rough or from various hilly lies.

That said, align your clubhead and yourself to the target, if anything shading your alignment slightly to the right of the hole. Usually, the rough will not grab the hosel of a wood as much as it will the thinner hosel of an iron, but there is still a tendency for the face to close slightly, so plan for this likelihood. Play the ball two inches back from where you would for a shot with this club from the fairway, so your hands are a touch ahead of the ball at address. You'll want to make contact just before the bottom of your swing, just as you would with an iron, to reduce the effect of the rough at impact.

Player A makes good contact and the ball comes out of the rough nicely, but he's pulled the shot a hair. The ball carries the left bunker and he hopes it will hold the green; but instead, since it's a little hot, it lands at the left edge of the green and bounds over the back-left, well past pin-high and in deep rough. His ball is 25 feet off the green and 60 feet from the hole. The lie looks reasonably good.

You'll need a great touch shot to save your par here. It's hard to tell how the ball will come out of the rough, and once it lands on the green, it will run downhill on the fast green. A soft shot with your sand wedge or, preferably, your lob wedge is what's called for.

Player A sets up. He aligns his body well left of the hole, positions the ball opposite his left heel, sets the face of a lob wedge wide open above the grass, and grips the very top end of the club. Next, he makes a smooth, extra-long, extra-loose wristy backswing. He drops the clubhead on a spot just behind the ball, causing it to pop out and float softly into the air. But because he catches the ball too cleanly, it lands on the green and runs 30 feet by the hole.

Player A two-putts for bogey.

COMMON STRATEGIC AND SHOTMAKING ERRORS BY THE A PLAYER

- Not planning tee shots on dogleg holes correctly
- Not grounding the club to "read" the lie on greenside chips and pitches

Butch's Lessons

Your technique was impressive, but you lacked some technical smarts that I'll give you a lesson on. You hit a good tee shot and didn't get rewarded because you didn't figure on the angle that this fairway takes in the landing area and also the fact that the tee ball tends to kick left upon landing. The result is that you drove it through the fairway. On this hole, with your length you need to start a ball a little right of center with a slight fade. This would allow the ball to land in the right half of the fairway so that even with the fairway bending right and the terrain sliding left, you'd keep that good tee shot in the fairway.

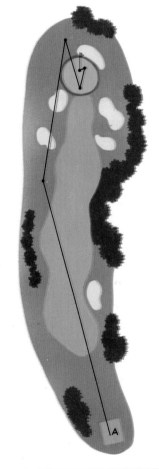

Here's a great tip for greenside "flop" shots: Most golfers hover the club above the grass behind the ball. Instead, ground your club an inch or two behind it. Grounding the sole of your lob wedge will help you measure how the ball is sitting in the grass. Sometimes, it sits up more than you think, as was the case here. The tendency will be to cut under it, so you need to apply a little more force in the swing than if the ball is sitting down. By soling your wedge, you'll get a better idea where the base of the ball is.

The B Player

This is a very tough par 4 for shorter drivers. Under normal conditions with no particular wind, the best you can hope for with a driver is to make it to the top of the hill, 230 yards away. This would leave you with a fairly level lie for a long second shot to the green.

Go with your driver here. There is no real advantage to laying up for you either, other than the fact that your odds of hitting the fairway are higher with a shorter club. But your good drive here would still give you a chance to get home in two, so you should take it.

Player B hits a solid drive in a quiet left-to-right fade pattern. His ball holds the right-center of the fairway, and he's left with a level lie. He now has 210 yards to the front edge, 225 yards to the middle of the green, and 235 yards to the hole, but the shot is downhill and will play 10 yards shorter. By the expression on Player B's face, I can tell that he's wondering if he should try to get home.

Yes, you should go for the green in two. You have hit a great drive, and you need to carry your second shot the equivalent of 200 yards to get to the front of the green. You can make the distance with a well-hit 3-wood. The big bunkers in front of the green extend well back from the front edge, so if you were to lay up you'd have to lay up well short of the green, leaving a fairly long pitch and run. This is a time you should go for it.

Unfortunately, Player B comes off the shot a bit, flying it low and sliding to the right, so that it never has a chance of clearing that big front-right bunker. Granted, he had to hit two perfect shots to make it home, and he only got one of the two. Now he faces a tough shot—a long bunker shot, about 35 yards, to a pin on the back level of the green with another bunker behind it.

Regarding your setup and execution for the long bunker shot, align both yourself and your clubhead more squarely to the target than you would for a shorter sand shot. This will help you swing the sand wedge along the target line, with the clubface less lofted, so that the same amount of swing force will give you a shot that comes out lower and longer, as you need here. Focus on a spot one to two inches behind the ball and swing down and through the sand firmly. Never try to pick the ball cleanly out of the sand, as that's an extremely risky shot—even when the lip is low. (On even longer bunker shots, of over 50 yards, try hitting a pitching wedge or even a 9-iron, opening the blade just slightly and making your normal swing.)

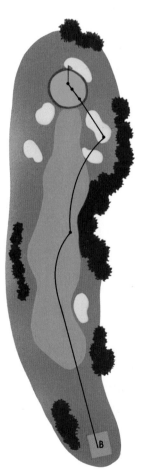

Regarding your strategy: You'll have to hit a perfect long bunker shot to carry the ball all the way to the hole. My recommendation: Plan instead on hitting the shot to the middle level of the green and trying for two putts from there. If you carry the shot a little farther than you figured and/or the ball releases more than you thought it would, it may well run up onto the top tier so that you have a good chance to make a par putt. But you should figure that as a bonus. You're better off planning on a well-executed but unforced shot that gets as far up into the green as possible. This should take some pressure off you.

Player B sets up perfectly, but because he lacks feel for distance, he fails to swing hard enough. The ball just reaches the green.

Your putt is not an easy one. Look at it from the top tier as well as from behind your ball, to give you a better feel for the force needed to get the ball to the hole. Usually you'll need to hit this putt a little harder than it looks.

Player B makes a good stroke, and the putt looks good, but comes up 8 feet short.

Take your time; the putt shouldn't have much break if any, and in these cases it's usually best to keep the ball "inside the hole" and stroke it firmly. You make it, and walk off with a bogey 5. That's really the same as parring it from the members' tees, so you've done well.

COMMON STRATEGIC AND SHOTMAKING ERRORS BY THE B PLAYER

- Bad feel for distance on long bunker shots
- Leaving uphill putts short

Before stepping into the sand to play a long bunker shot, make practice swings in the grass. This routine will give you a feel for the proper swinging action and the correct tempo.

Butch's Lessons

The long sand shot is a tough one for anybody. The tendency is to try to scoop the ball out. Play this shot pretty much like you would off the fairway. But get a feel first for the length and tempo of swing needed by taking a few practice swings in the grass outside the bunker.

On uphill putts, it pays to imagine a second hole a couple of feet behind the real one. This mental image will help you stroke the ball more firmly, so you "get up."

The C Player

Decide right off the bat to play this hole as a par 5. Under normal conditions, even with your best drive you won't be able to get home in two here. So, there's no reason to press on either your tee shot or second shot.

I recommend taking a 3-wood off the tee. Especially given your tendency to slice, aim for the left side of the fairway. Stay compact and smooth going back, then release the club freely.

Player C gets under the ball slightly, so that he fails to achieve maximum distance. In fact, he's only 170 yards out in the left-center of the fairway.

You still have a long way to the green, so you want to hit a smart second and set up an open third to the green. The two fairway bunkers I mentioned earlier guard the fairway near the landing area for your second shot. If you hit the ball straight, of course, they are no problem. However, a slight pull or push with a 3-wood could put you in one of them.

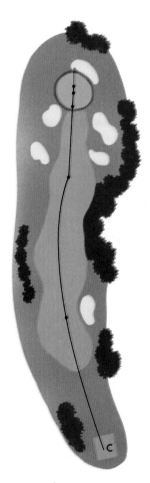

I think the smarter play is to play a position shot, well short of the green, but in the fairway. This is the perfect time to take out your 7-wood. Line up the shot with care, then just make a nice, smooth swing.

Player C follows my instructions, and lands the ball in the fairway, just short of the bunkers and about 110 yards from the pin.

You have plenty of green to work with. You might be able to get to the pin with a full pitching wedge. However, with the pin on the back level, a much better bet is to take out an 8- or 9-iron and play a lower, more controlled shot in. You want to land the ball just below the top level, from where it will hopefully skitter up to the level the pin is on. Play the ball from a narrow stance that's just a touch open, with the ball centered and your hands ahead. Make a swing that feels three-quarters in length and hit down and through decisively, keeping your wrists firm.

Player C follows my directions to the letter, except he doesn't accelerate the club fast enough in the impact zone and comes up well short. Nevertheless, on the plus side, the ball is on the green, albeit 35 feet from the hole.

Player C takes his time reading the break and rehearsing the stroke he intends to put on the ball. His preswing work pays off; two putts for bogey, which is his personal "par."

COMMON STRATEGIC AND SHOTMAKING ERRORS BY THE C PLAYER

- "Skying" the tee shot
- Leaving a pitch short

If you're looking to hit drives lower, so the ball runs farther once it lands, play the ball opposite your left heel. Only when looking to carry the ball longer in the air should you position it forward of that spot.

Butch's Lessons

Many amateurs, just like you, tend to move the ball up in their stance too far when they are looking for more distance off the tee. One chief reason you hit a weak sky was that you had the ball positioned opposite your left toe. No pro plays it there. In fact, many play the ball behind the standard left heel position. But they hit hundreds of practice balls each day. You'll make solid contact if you just move it back, opposite your left heel.

To prevent hitting pitch shots short of the hole, focus on the top of the flag. I find this helps me fly the ball all the way to the hole. Simply looking at the hole encourages you to land the ball well short of the pin.

HOLE	1	2	3	4	5	6	7	8	9	OUT	
YARDS	366	380	485	177	368	373	103	515	356	3123	
PAR	4	4	5	3	4	4	3	5	4	36	
Player A	5	5	5	3	3	4	3	5	4	37	
Player B	5	6	5	4	5	5	4	5	4	43	
Player C	6	4	8	4	5	5	5	6	4	47	

HOLE	10	11	12	13	14	15	16	17	18	IN	TOTAL
YARDS	183	508	121	339	339	417	407	452	510	3276	6399
PAR	3	5	3	4	4	4	4	4	5	36	72
Player A	3	5	3	3	5	5	5	5			
Player B	3	5	3	4	6	4	5	5			
Player C	4	6	4	5	5	4	4	5			

WESTCHESTER COUNTRY CLUB
Par 5: 510 yards

The West Course at Westchester Country Club is highly underrated. Designed by Walter J. Travis in 1922, and located in the New York City suburb of Rye, it is not usually rated a world-class course, but maybe it should be, for it remains one of the most challenging layouts in America. I'm not alone in my opinion, either; even though Westchester is not recognized by the leading magazines, pros like and respect it very much.

Since 1972, the West Course has hosted the Westchester Classic, and for most of those years the championship was held the week before the United States Open. Professionals such as Jack Nicklaus, the inaugural winner of the event, used to like playing in this tournament—namely, because the tough conditions helped ready them for the Open.

Like Garden City, another famous Travis design, Westchester is not an exceptionally long course. It plays to well under 7000 yards from the members' tees, yet the course is testy. Featuring relatively narrow hilly fairways bordered by pines, oaks, and maples, small undulating fast greens, deep bunkers, and penal rough, the West demands that golfers play target golf.

Travis, a world-class amateur who had played golf on the most famous courses of his native Australia and in America and England, won both the American and British Amateur championships. He had a great appreciation for what elements of a golf course players would like and dislike.

One of the things that many club-level players dislike, or perhaps fear, is a dogleg-left hole. The main reason is, most amateurs slice. Travis, who himself was a very straight hitter, thought that all golfers should learn to make driving accuracy a priority over driving distance, so he included several dogleg-left holes in his West Course. Each of these requires the player to hit either a controlled draw around the corner or a power-fade that starts down the left and finishes in the center or right-center of the fairway.

A classic example of a challenging dogleg-left hole

is the par-5 18th, 510 yards from the men's middle tees. Made famous by Bob Gilder, who holed out a 251-yard 3-wood shot for a double-eagle 2 during the 1982 Westchester Classic, the 18th fairway is bordered by rough and trees practically all the way from tee to green. To make things tougher, the green itself features traps left, right, and behind the green, plus heavy rough beyond the first cut of tightly mowed fringe grass. The putting surface slopes upward from front to back, so that if the pin is on the rear tier, and you're behind the hole, you face a gut-wrenching shot. Let's play this great finishing hole together, so that you know what to do when facing a hole of similar design.

The A Player

This hole is perfectly designed for you, particularly since you possess the rare ability to hit a power-draw around the corner. Such a drive allows you to actually shorten the hole and face a relatively straightforward wood shot into the green. And if you do get home, you'll have a good chance to score eagle.

When I saw you steer the swing and block your tee shot into the right rough, I knew that you were protecting against hitting a duck-hook. Whenever you fear the duck-hook, the natural thing is to grip more tightly and fail to release the arms, hands, and club fluidly. Instead of coming into the ball with the clubhead moving at maximum speed, the tendency is to decelerate and leave the clubface open. Now, tell me what you plan to do with this second shot.

No, put that middle iron away. You don't need to play a safe shot here. I know the ball is sitting down slightly, but you can blast the ball down the fairway by using a 4-wood, and playing a powerful cut-shot that my dad taught me—and Ben Hogan.

Start from a very open stance, aiming about 30 yards left of the green. Position the ball just behind your left heel, turn your left foot out more than normal, and lay the clubface wide open. Also, grip more firmly than normal, so that you prevent the grass from closing the clubface at impact.

The 4-wood cut-shot: address.

The 4-wood cut-shot: backswing.

The 4-wood cut-shot: downswing.

Keep your backswing action upright and compact, and take the club slightly outside the target line.

Pull the club down into the back of the ball; "just beat on it," as my dad used to tell me.

Because you will cut across the ball, it will fly higher than normal in a fade pattern, and thus sit down more quickly. So, you don't have to worry about the ball bouncing wildly or running hard into a bunker.

Player A followed my directions perfectly, landing the ball short of the green. From there, he hit a sand wedge 35 feet above the hole and two-putted for par.

COMMON STRATEGIC AND SHOTMAKING ERRORS BY THE A PLAYER

- Not planting a positive thought in his mind before hitting the tee shot
- Not setting himself up for a makable birdie putt

Butch's Lessons

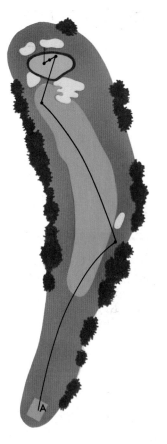

You steered the swing and hit the drive into the deep rough on the right because you pictured hitting a snap-hook. Or you told yourself not to hit the ball left, then defensively hit it well right of target.

Make a habit of always planting a positive image or thought into your mind just before you swing. In this case, you should have imagined the ball curving around the dogleg, then landing in the short grass on the left side of the fairway. When you see it hooking dramatically into trouble on the left side, you'll simply hit it there, or guard against that by going the other way. Nicklaus has always said that he never missed a shot in his head before he swung. Maybe that's why he mishit fewer shots than any golfer who ever played the game. This mental attitude may not make you play as well as Jack did during his heyday, but I guarantee it will help you hit fewer bad shots and lower your handicap.

Knowing that the green slopes downward from the back, on your wedge shot you should have done everything you could to keep the ball below the cup. I recommend that the next time you face a similar situation, you play a pitching wedge rather than a sand wedge. Because this club features less loft than the sand iron, it will allow you to land the ball farther back on the green so that it runs up to the hole. Many smart course strategists feed the ball to the hole; in this case, you should do that, so that you leave yourself an uphill putt. By going past the hole, you were unable to charge the putt, since you had to worry about hitting the ball well by the hole and three-putting. As it turned out, you hit the ball so softly that you nearly three-putted anyway. Learn from this strategic error, and practice hitting pitching-wedge shots from around the green.

The B Player

Your priority here is to just hit the fairway. Because your natural shot is a fade, anywhere in the short grass is fine. Ideally, however, you will want to start the ball down the left side of the fairway and let it drift right slightly. From there, you can hit a fairway wood shot down in front of the green, and be in position to score birdie.

Player B aims his ball down the center of the fairway, and is lucky that the ball doesn't land in the right rough. Still, the breaks even out during a round, and the secret is to take advantage of them. He does just that, taking a 3-wood out and smashing it solidly down the fairway, approximately 80 yards short of the green.

In perfect position, he also could have chosen to feed the ball to the hole with a pitching wedge, but instead plays an overaggressive sand-wedge approach. In fact, he attacks the flag, and the ball finishes over the green in the thick grass. Fortunately, the ball is sitting up. Unfortunately, he employs a technique more suited to hitting a shot out of a bad lie. He sets most of his weight on his left foot, keeps his hands ahead of the ball through impact, and hits down too hard. It's a good thing he slows his swing down to the point of reaching maximum deceleration through impact, because he hits the grass under the ball causing it to pop straight up in the air—so much so that the ball never reaches the green. From there, he plays a good chip, and 1 putts for a bogey 6.

I applaud you for keeping your cool after fluffing that mini-pitch shot from behind the green. Still, you made a couple of silly mistakes I'd like to talk to you about.

- Poor aiming strategy off the tee
- Playing the wrong shot from behind the green

Butch's Lessons

You're going to have to face a heck of a lot more tee shots like the one on the 18th hole at Westchester, shots that require you to aim down the left side of the fairway and work the ball back to its center. To help ensure that you hit the ball at your initial target, pick an interim spot along your aiming line, about three feet in front of the ball. Next, set the clubface square to it.

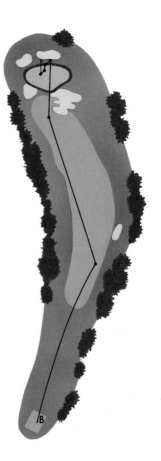

In playing a high, soft greenside shot from a good lie, accelerate your arms on the downswing, and hold the clubface open through impact.

Knowing that you are aimed correctly will also heighten your confidence and help you employ a smoother swing.

You must develop a more expansive repertoire of greenside shots. The only way to do this is practice. So, if you are really serious about improving, sacrifice some playing time for some practice time, and hit some chips and pitches at the course or in your backyard.

In hitting a short shot like the one you faced from the rough behind the green, with the ball sitting up, try the following technique:

Play the ball off your left heel, in an open stance.

Set your hands slightly behind the ball, with the clubface in a slightly open position.

Make a compact backswing almost entirely with your arms.

Swing through, accelerating the arms and trying to keep the clubface pointing toward the sky through impact.

Actions like these will allow you to float the ball all the way to the hole, so that it sits down practically immediately after hitting the green.

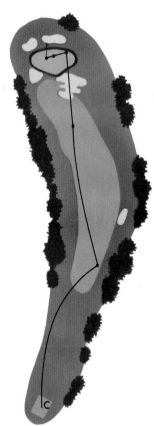

The C Player

If the tee shot on this hole presents psychological problems for the B player, who normally fades the ball, you can imagine what a difficult hole this is for the C player, who often slices. Still, it can be conquered. The secrets to eliminating slices are concentrating intently and swinging smoothly.

The C player starts his tee shot as far left as he can without hitting the trees, to give himself maximum room for his natural slice. From there he plays a nice fairway wood shot that fades slightly and lands about 110 yards short of the green.

Player C becomes so excited by his second shot that he's anxious to hit his third and maybe score a birdie. Failing to keep his emotions on an even keel, he rushes his preshot routine and hits only a middling 9-iron to the back right edge of the green. A good lag putt and a solid short putt help him score par.

- Having to play for a slice
- Rushing his routine on his third shot

Butch's Lessons

I commend you on the way you played for your slice. However, this is a shot you want to work on correcting. Right now, your swing is much too upright, and you swing the club from outside in.

DRILL (FOR FLATTENING OUT A STEEP SWING PLANE)

Assume your normal stance for a driver. Now, instead of grounding the club, hold it at chest level, then extend your arms outward. Swing. Feel the flatness of the plane. Yes, it's close to a baseball swing.

Next, lower the club a few inches, then swing.

Keep lowering the club, until the clubhead is at ground level, with its face square to the ball.

Swing. It will feel nice to swing the club on a more rounded plane, and on an inside-square-inside path, plus hit solid shots.

Whenever you get into a slice slump, work on this drill. It will also help you rotate your arms in a counterclockwise direction through impact. This type of release will allow you to turn a slice into a draw, and pick up yardage rather than lose it.

Even though you hold a high handicap, you could have hit a better third shot just by taking more time to line up. You rushed your routine, instead of taking the time to make sure you squared the clubface to an interim spot left of the flag. In the future, stand behind the ball before setting up. Take a smooth practice swing while staring at your initial aiming spot, then step to the ball and square up to it.

HOLE	1	2	3	4	5	6	7	8	9	OUT	
YARDS	366	380	485	177	368	373	103	515	356	3123	
PAR	4	4	5	3	4	4	3	5	4	36	
Player A	5	5	5	3	3	4	3	5	4	37	
Player B	5	6	5	4	5	5	4	5	4	43	
Player C	6	4	8	4	5	5	5	6	4	47	
HOLE	10	11	12	13	14	15	16	17	18	IN	TOTAL
YARDS	183	508	121	339	339	417	407	452	510	3276	6399
PAR	3	5	3	4	4	4	4	4	5	36	72
Player A	3	5	3	3	5	5	5	5	5	39	76
Player B	3	5	3	4	6	4	5	5	6	41	84
Player C	4	6	4	5	5	4	4	5	5	42	89

THE 19TH HOLE

Well, gentlemen, here's to the round—cheers! I really enjoyed going around 18 holes with all of you.

I think all three of you played well, but as I tell even Tiger Woods, there's always room for improvement. And there's no better place to discuss just a few things about your games than here at Seminole Golf Club in North Palm Beach, Florida, my favorite of all 19th holes.

Player A, a few mental errors cost you strokes today, so I'd like you to concentrate harder on developing smart strategic habits. Take more time to consider the layout of the hole, visualize more intently the shot you intend to play—either off the tee or into a green—and discipline yourself to play the percentages.

Player B, skillwise, you're not that far from being a single-figure-handicap scorer on a regular basis. Yet, you'd certainly lower your handicap faster if you learned how to play a controlled draw. Therefore, practice what I taught you.

Player C, you learned a whole lot in just one round. Still, you and I both know that the fastest way for you to raise the level of your game is to groove good setup fundamentals by working on the keys we discussed. A better grasp of the elements of grip, stance, ball position, posture, aim and alignment will surely help you cure your slice.

Good luck, and if you have a problem with your game, don't hesitate to call me at the Rio Hotel in Las Vegas, Nevada. I'd be more than happy to give you a lesson at my new home base.

INDEX

Note to the reader: Page numbers for illustration captions are set in italics.

at Shinnecock Hills, 15
at Shoal Creek, 118
sloping, 161
thinking about going for, 139-40,
    141
"Green light" situation, 47, *173*
Greenside chips and pitches, ground-
    ing club on, 204-6
Greenside sand shots, 90
Greenside shots, technique for, 219-
    220, *219*
Greenside technique
    right, *39*
    wrong, 38
"Grind mode," 101
Grip
    pressure, 28
    in sand, *36*
    tension, and slicing driver, 27-28
    weak, and controlled fade, 192,
        192
    See also Strong grip

Hands
    -arm-club release, 91, *93*
    and downswing, 103
    pulling club inside with, 122, *122*
    release of, 174
Harmon, Claude, 84
Harmon, Craig, 201, 202
Headwind, 87
Heel hits, off tee, 162, 163, 164
High finish position, 175, *176*
High-handicappers, 115
    approach shots by, 166
    and perfect shot, 178
    poor execution by, 92
    shooting themselves in foot, 91
    and strong grip, 113-14
    See also C player
High shots, as errors, 65-66, 89, 90
Hitting down, in deep rough, 123-25,
    124
Hogan, Ben, 27, 32, 33, 36, 83, 151,
    189, 215
Hole
    dogleg, 205
    dogleg-left, 214-15
    fighting design of, 192-93

Hooking tee shots, 175-78, *176*
Hoylake course (Britain), 56

Inverness Club
    character of, 106
    greens of, 106, 107
    hole 8 at, 105, 106-16
    location of, 105
    origin as nine-hole course, 105
    par (official) for hole 8 at, 105, 116
    remodeling of, 105
    yards (official) for hole 8 at, 105,
        116
Iron(s)
    blasting out of sand, *173*
    blocked, 163
    lofted, controlled shot with, *26*
    long, swinging with, 194-96
    short, and approach shots, 111-12
    soft shots with, 73
    toe hits with, 49-50
Irons, types of
    2-iron, 159-60
    3-iron, 34, 171, 194-95
    4-iron, 61, 89, 129
    5-iron, 37, 48-50, 129, 157-58, 174
    6-iron, 35, 120, 165-66
    7-iron, 22, 88, 114, 131, 165-66,
        192
    8-iron, 72, 111, 162, 197
    9-iron, 39, 142, 151, 159-60, 171-
        172, 178, 196, 197, 220
Iron shots
    and knee-flex, retaining, 77
    "pressing," 37-38
    slowing down swing on, 38
    swing, overly compact, on, 153-54,
        153
Irwin, Hale, 100, 128, 169

Jones, Bobby, 189
Jones, Robert Trent, 33

Knee. *See* Left knee
Knee-flex, retaining in hitting area,
    77, *77*

Lay-up shot, 139, 178-79
    with draw flight, 47-48, *47*

CLAUDE "BUTCH" HARMON, JR., is best known as the teacher of Tiger Woods. The Director of the Butch Harmon School of Golf at the Rio Secco Golf Club in Las Vegas, Nevada, Harmon is the author of *The Four Cornerstones of Winning Golf.* Harmon is the son of Claude Harmon, Sr., the 1948 Masters champion.

JOHN ANDRISANI is consulting editor at *Golf Magazine.* A former golf instructor, Andrisani has written books with the game's top pros and teachers. Most recently, he authored *The Tiger Woods Way: Secrets of Tiger Woods' Power-Swing Technique,* and coauthored *The Four Cornerstones of Winning Golf* with Butch Harmon.

ALLEN WELKIS is a multiple award-winning artist whose illustrations have appeared in *Golf Magazine* and in the book *The Tiger Woods Way: Secrets of Tiger Woods' Power-Swing Technique.* Welkis lives in Fort Salonga, New York.

LEONARD KAMSLER is a staff photographer at *Golf Magazine* whose work has also appeared in several golf books. He is a resident of New York City.